How to Talk to Children about

TOM QUINLAN

twentythirdpublications.com

Second printing 2018

Cover illustration: ©iStockphoto.com / KanKhem

TWENTY-THIRD PUBLICATIONS
One Montauk Avenue, Suite 200
New London, CT 06320
(860) 437-3012 or (800) 321-0411
www.twentythirdpublications.com

ISBN: 978-1-62785-309-5
Printed in the U.S.A.

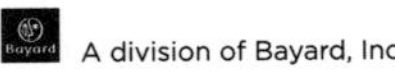
A division of Bayard, Inc.

Introduction

"How do I talk to my child about...?" This is not an uncommon question among parents as well as teachers and catechists. Abstract concepts, hard-to-broach subjects, and sensitive issues all require a particular kind of language that gives a child enough information without being overly complex or confusing. The same is true for aspects of our faith. How do we talk to children about the great big concept of God or about the life, ministry, death, and resurrection of Jesus? How do we explain the gestures, symbols, and ritual of the Mass or approach issues of morality and making sound choices?

This series of books provides parents as well as teachers and catechists with a range of questions about these topics. Each one offers terminology relatable to a young child's experience as well as family activities to stimulate further conversation and comprehension. In sharing these responses, you are likely to find yourself more than capable of talking to your child about these and other topics of faith and practice.

Why do we call it "Mass"?

For your information

In the Latin Mass, the prayer of dismissal contains the word *missa*, which conveys a sense of going on mission. The mission on which each of us is sent is the same mission Jesus sent his disciples to accomplish. We are to bring *good news* (which means *gospel*) of the saving love of our God to all people!

A more ancient term for Catholic worship is *liturgy*. In Greek, it means "work of the people," and early Christians adopted it to describe their worship. The word is used today to describe various structured (or ritualized) worship services. The Mass, for example, has two major structures: Liturgy of the Word and Liturgy of the Eucharist.

Mass (or liturgy) is the prayer of all of us. We should give our full self in this great prayer. We sing and respond and offer our hearts and minds. The *body of Christ* (as St. Paul calls us) gathers, celebrates, and is then sent forth to be the presence of Jesus in the world. By helping children learn the songs and responses and by your own active participation, you are encouraging their participation in the Mass.

Talking with your child

First, help your child understand that Jesus came to bring the good news (gospel) of his Father in heaven to the world. Ask your child what this good news could be. It's a really important question. Here are some key points for discussing this:

- God loves us all...so much that he became human!

- Jesus brings a special message of hope to all of us, but especially to the poor, the outcast, and the sick.
- Jesus proves that we have nothing to fear, even from death itself.
- Through the suffering, death, and resurrection of Jesus, God offers us forgiveness, joy in this life, and life eternal in heaven.

Jesus then invites us, his disciples, to help him share the good news with others. Ask your child how your family can share the good news of Jesus with people you know. Try to name specific ways you each already do this. (Hint: It's about *both* what we say *and* what we do.)

ACTION STEP
Name people who might need to hear and experience the good news that Jesus wants us to share. Together, think of something you can do this week to bring the gospel to them.

When we bring the good news of Jesus to others, we are sharing in his mission, his purpose. Explain that in an old language (Latin), the word for *mission* is related to the word *Mass*. And so, when we leave Mass, we should be ready to do the holy work of God out in the world!

Listen with your children to the last words, the dismissal, at Mass, and talk about what it means. (Dismissal rite options include: "Go and announce the Gospel of the Lord" and "Go in peace, glorifying the Lord by your life.")

Prayer

Father God, you sent your Son, Jesus, to share the good news that you love and save us. And now you ask us to be followers of Jesus and helpers in his mission. Open our hearts to say "yes" always to what you ask of us. Amen.

Is that the Bible they are reading from up there?

For your information

The book is called a "lectionary" and it contains many passages from Scripture. However, it is not the Bible.

The Catholic Church and many other Christian faith traditions use the same lectionary. Its purpose is to make sure that the most important readings from Scripture are proclaimed over time. The readings are set out in a pattern to match the themes of the liturgical (church) year. So, for example, in Advent we hear readings about getting ready for Jesus.

There is a Sunday lectionary, which has a three-year cycle, with an emphasis on the gospels of Matthew, Mark, and Luke, respectively. (John's gospel is spread throughout the cycle.) You'll notice that when you listen to the Sunday readings at Mass, there is usually a connection between the first reading and the gospel reading. There is also a weekday lectionary with a two-year cycle, for use at daily Mass.

Because the Church uses the lectionary, the same readings are proclaimed in every Catholic Church in the world every Sunday. This is a sign of our unity as Catholics.

Talking to your child

Ask what your child understands about the Bible. (This is more than just what they know *from* the Bible.) Here are some valuable points to share:

- The Bible is not a book. It is a collection of various forms of writing (letters, stories, poems, history, etc.) gathered over the course of centuries.

ACTION STEP Try spending some time each week in family prayer that includes reading the gospel passage proclaimed at Sunday Mass. (Sunday evening might be a good time.) Then give everyone a chance to share what they think the Scripture means and how each person feels called to live out the passage this week. (There are many ways to get the lectionary readings for Sundays and weekdays, including the internet and apps.)

Create a prayerful setting for this family time. Have a special place in your home to gather, with a crucifix or image of Jesus, a Bible, and perhaps personal items of faith. You can light a candle to help your children experience the word of God as light for your family.

- We call the Bible the "word of God." This means that while human beings produced these writings, God provided inspiration to make sure that the writings communicate divine truth.
- The Bible contains the Hebrew Scriptures (known as the Old Testament), which is about all that happened before Jesus.
- The Bible contains the New Testament, which is about Jesus and the early church.

Now explain that the big book up front in church is called a "lectionary" and that it contains special readings selected from the Bible for us to hear every Sunday (and even daily). Encourage them to listen carefully at Mass to see if they can find connections among the readings at Mass and the connection to the season we are celebrating in the life of the Church.

Prayer

God, the Father, you sent Jesus to proclaim your word. Open our ears and hearts so that we can understand your message and live out your truth each time we read from or listen to Scripture. Amen.

What's that really long prayer we say?

For your information

At the end of the Liturgy of the Word (the first half of Mass), we stand to recite together a formal statement of Catholic faith, a creed. Parishes have the option to use the Apostles' Creed, which is a shorter creed. Most parishes use the lengthier Nicene Creed.

The Nicene Creed originates from the Council of Nicaea (in Turkey) in 325 AD, pulling together pieces of early Christian faith. It was the work of the bishops at that council to formalize the key aspects of faith into one statement to help to unite all Christians. It helped to clarify that Jesus is as much God as the Father is God. (When we say "consubstantial with the Father," we are affirming the full divinity of Jesus.)

This Creed was developed further at a bishops' council in 381 and remains the primary statement of Catholic faith for the world today. Most non-Catholic Christians also use the Creed.

Talking to your child

Explain to your children that what we recite after the homily is not really a prayer. It is a very old expression of Christian faith that we all believe as members of the Church. The word for a statement of faith is *creed.*

Share that our Catholic Creed is often referred to as the *Profession of Faith* at Mass. When we say it out loud with everyone else at Mass, the Creed is a powerful sign of our unity as believers. We should say it with confidence and gratitude. Find out which Creed (either Nicene or Apostles') is recited as the Profession of Faith at your parish. Make copies of that Creed for study with your children at home. Read through it together and help your children understand the meaning of particular statements of faith within it. If you don't understand certain elements of the Creed, consult a trustworthy source in your family, the parish, or online. Consider owning a copy of the *Catechism of the Catholic Church* for family reference.

Ask your children to see if they can find a basic structure to the creed. Can you recognize it? (Hint: It has three major parts.)

Both the Nicene and Apostles' Creeds have a Trinitarian structure. This means that the Creed is broken into parts about each person of the Trinity: the Father, the Son, and the Holy Spirit. Faith in the Trinity, while not explicitly expressed in the Bible, was a central belief of early Christianity and remains so today. This creedal structure helps to teach about the Trinity and explain the different roles each of the three Persons of God plays in our world.

ACTION STEP Make a point of reciting the Creed as a family at Mass. Model for your children the voicing of this Profession of Faith with conviction and pride. As needed, help your children to read the words on the page in the worship aid used at your parish. And consider practicing and discussing the Creed at home.

Prayer

God of all knowledge, through the Church you share your saving truth with us. We praise you for this gift and ask your help in coming to know you better and better. Amen.

What is brought forward during Mass?

For your information

The Presentation of the Gifts is a part of the Mass that shifts us from the Liturgy of the Word to the Liturgy of the Eucharist. It is proper that members of the faith community come forward to present the gifts of bread and wine to the celebrant, the priest celebrating the Mass. This food symbolically represents *us*. In poetic terms, each of us brings our grain of wheat and grape and adds it to the making of these gifts that the priest receives on God's behalf.

For ancient cultures, *sacrifice* was an important religious ritual. In Israelite practice, first fruits of the land, whether grain or an animal, were often brought to a sacrificial altar for destruction by fire. The intention in such religious sacrifice was that God would find the offering acceptable and continue to bless the people.

The sacrificial dynamic at Mass is a radical departure from this. What we offer God as a gift representing our lives ends up coming *back* to us as the ultimate gift of Jesus in the Eucharist. Jesus dying on the cross was the final sacrifice, and at Mass we are connecting to its power through the meal Jesus commanded us to eat.

Talking to your child

Come early to Mass next Sunday and spend a few moments in the back of the church showing the hosts and the wine to your child. Ask if your child would like to bring them up to the priest some Sunday at Mass. (All you have to do is ask the usher.) Help your child understand that

- the bread and wine are not special or different yet.

- the bread and wine are in the back of the church so that members of the parish can help bring them before God.

- people from long ago used to offer gifts to make God happy.

- the only gift that God wants from us now is the gift of our lives.

- each time we pray, including at Mass, we have a chance to offer our hearts and lives to God.

ACTION STEP Talk about how much God loves us. Each member of the family can name signs of God's generosity in their life. What might be some ways, individually and together, your family can make an acceptable gift of your lives to God? Perhaps your family can decide on appropriate sacrifices of time and possessions and comforts that can be lifted up as a prayer of gratitude.

In addition to the bread and wine brought forward to become the Eucharist, your child may wonder about the money that is collected. The *Offertory* occurs when the financial gifts of individuals and families are gathered to benefit the parish and the needy. Teach your children that parishes are able to serve the mission of Christ through the gifts of people's time and talent and also financial treasure. We are invited to give in response to God's great generosity in our lives.

Prayer

Gracious God, we have so much to be thankful for, and we give you our praise and worship. We lift up our lives and offer them to you. Please continue to bless us and others in your goodness. Amen.

When did the first Mass happen?

For your information

So much of Christianity has its origins in Judaism. For this reason we use the term *Judeo-Christian tradition* to describe our roughly 4,000 years of history.

The Catholic Mass traces its roots back to two religious expressions: 1) the Jewish Scripture service conducted in synagogues during Jesus' time, which developed into the Christian Liturgy of the Word, and 2) the Christian sacrificial meal commemorating the suffering, death, and resurrection of Jesus.

The Eucharist was instituted by Jesus himself on the night before he died. Jesus and his disciples had gathered to celebrate the Jewish Passover. In this Passover meal, Jews remember how God took action to rescue his people from slavery and bring them to freedom. In the Eucharistic meal we ritually celebrate God's action, in the suffering, death, and resurrection of Jesus, which offers us passage from death to life. We call this passage the *paschal mystery*.

Talking to your child

Help your child understand that what we do during the Liturgy of the Eucharist was created by Jesus at the Last Supper. Explain that Jesus knew he was going to die the next day and wanted to have a way to stay close to his friends (and all of us).

Jesus and his apostles, who were Jewish, gathered that night for the special Jewish holiday called *Passover*. They celebrated Passover and remembered the history of God's goodness to the Jewish people. But Jesus also did something new and amazing at this meal.

The gospels tell us that Jesus took the bread on the table and blessed it and gave it to his friends, saying, "This is my Body." And then he took the cup with wine and blessed it and gave it, saying, "This is the cup of my Blood." The apostles ate and drank of this food, which was the first meal that we call *Eucharist.*

ACTION STEP Plan to attend a Passover Seder meal. This is what Jesus and his apostles gathered for on the night of the Last Supper. If you know Jewish people, consider asking if they might welcome your family to participate with them. Also, many parishes provide a Seder Meal experience in Lent to help us better understand the close relationship between the Jewish and Christian faiths.

Discuss what we do in the second half of Mass, the Liturgy of the Eucharist, and how it follows what happened at the Last Supper. We do what Jesus did in response to his command. And we do it to have Jesus close to us in the meal that is his Body and Blood. The Eucharist is our "Bread of Life."

Impress upon your child that every time we go to Mass and go to communion, we are receiving this precious gift of Eucharist that Jesus created for his followers. In the Eucharist we receive Jesus in a very close and powerful way, with us and in us!

Prayer

God and Father of all, you first rescued your special Jewish people. And then you gave us your Son, Jesus, as savior of the world. We give you our great thanks and ask you to bless all of us. Amen.

What is the priest doing at the altar?

For your information

After the gifts of bread and wine are presented from the assembly to the celebrant (the priest celebrating the Mass), he brings the bread and wine to the altar, and we begin the part of the Mass called the Liturgy of the Eucharist. (*Eucharist* comes from a Greek word for "thanksgiving.")

The celebrant selects a version of the Eucharistic Prayer in the *Roman Missal* (the large book on the altar) and begins to pray this great prayer of the Church. He calls the Holy Spirit down upon the bread and wine to change them into Christ's Body and Blood. After recalling Jesus' words and actions at the Last Supper, consecration of the Eucharist has occurred.

We kneel for the Eucharistic Prayer to show our deep reverence for what is happening in our presence. It is ancient, sacred worship. Note the "we" language in the Eucharistic Prayer. This is our collective prayer, and we are called to participate fully, with our heart, mind, voice, and body.

Talking to your child

Sometime at Mass, ask your child to be very observant during the Eucharistic Prayer. Say that you will be asking some questions afterward. (If your child has difficulty seeing, consider sitting toward the front of the church. Or, invite them to stand very reverently on the kneeler.) Try these questions (with a little help on the answers):

- Why do we kneel at this part of Mass? (*Something very important is happening.*)

- What should we be doing then? (*The priest is leading the prayer, but everyone in the church should be praying with the priest.*)

ACTION STEP
After Mass, gather as a family around the altar. Say a prayer of thanksgiving for the gift of the Eucharist. (The altar is a most sacred element in a Catholic church. Your family may reverently touch it.)

- What happens to the bread and wine that is brought up to the altar? (*By the power of God, it becomes the Body and Blood of Jesus. Or, the bread and wine change into the* real presence *of Jesus. By a miracle of God, Jesus is somehow* really *in the Eucharist.*)

- Why do we believe in the *real presence* of Jesus in the Eucharist? (For two good reasons: *Jesus said it* and *the earliest Christians believed it—believed in the real presence of Jesus in the Eucharist.*)

- Why is the Eucharist brought down from the altar for us to eat? (*Jesus wants to be close to us always and help us live happy, holy lives. This food, which is his Body and Blood, allows him to be with us in a very special, very close way.*)

If your child has not received First Eucharist yet, discuss what the Eucharist tastes like. Explain that the look and taste have not changed from bread and wine but that their inner substance has changed into Jesus in a way we can't fully understand.

Prayer

Loving Jesus, thank you so much for giving us the greatest gift ever in the Eucharist. May we always accept your gift with gratitude and joy. And may it help us to become more and more loving like you. Amen.

What's in that special box?

For your information

The tabernacle is where the leftover Eucharist is kept. Only the hosts are reserved, however. Any leftover Eucharist in the form (species) of wine is consumed at the end of the Communion Rite.

Extra hosts that have been consecrated are reserved for several possible uses. Ministers of care will bring Eucharist to those unable to attend Mass (in hospitals, in nursing homes, or in private homes). This is an ancient reason for reserving the Eucharist. Also a communion service would use reserved Eucharist.

There is reference to tabernacles in early church writings. From very early on, Christians were taking great care to ensure that the bread consecrated at the Eucharistic liturgy was being properly stored and protected. This shows how the first generations of Christians understood the Eucharist to be a real, sacramental presence of Jesus.

Talking to your child

During Mass, ask your child to watch the activity at the tabernacle. What is in it? Why do people act so carefully there and genuflect (bending one knee to the ground) in front of it? See what your child can infer by observation.

After Mass or at another time, approach the tabernacle as a family. Do so with great reverence, as this is one of the holiest places in a Catholic church. Explain that this is where leftover Eucharistic (communion) hosts are kept. Talk to your child about the uses for these hosts. Teach your child another name for the Eucharist: the Blessed Sacrament.

Ask your child why we genuflect in front of the tabernacle and take great care with the hosts contained within. Help your child to understand that, in a very real way, Jesus is present, right there in front of us, in the Eucharist being kept in the tabernacle. It is a special place!

ACTION STEP
Find a minister of care in the parish whom your family can accompany in delivering the Eucharist. The parish could assist with this. It is a beautiful ministry of bringing Jesus to those unable to attend Mass. Perhaps it is a ministry you might consider joining.

Point out the candle that is next to the tabernacle. Explain that any time the candle is lit, the Eucharist is in the tabernacle. (Eucharist is always kept in the tabernacle, with the exception of from late on Holy Thursday to the Easter Vigil Mass.)

Spend some time kneeling or standing in prayer in front of the tabernacle, close to the presence of the Blessed Sacrament. Develop a practice of spending time after Mass or during a special visit to church, kneeling and praying with a focus on the presence of Jesus in the tabernacle.

Also, be sure to teach your child the proper way to genuflect. When entering the pew at church (and again when leaving the pew after Mass), bend the right knee to the ground. One's sight and consciousness should be focused on the tabernacle. This is a Catholic ritual action that honors God and reminds us of Jesus' presence in the reserved Eucharist.

Prayer

Jesus, you feed us with your very Body and Blood. May we honor you always in this Blessed Sacrament, especially by being living tabernacles who carry you in us. Amen.

Why is there a pool (or bowl) of water in church?

For your information

Having had your child baptized not too many years ago, you know that the water container is called a *baptismal font* or pool.

In old churches you will probably find fonts that are small. They were built for use with infants and were more functional than symbolic. Since the reforms of the Second Vatican Council in the early 1960s, many newer churches have installed large pools designed for both infant and adult baptisms. The size of these baptismal pools also symbolically communicates the magnitude of God's saving power.

These newer baptismal pools are more like the ones of the first centuries of Christianity, when whole families were coming to faith in Jesus Christ and the adults were fully immersed in the water. Many parishes baptize adults this way today.

Baptism is a once-for-a-lifetime sacrament that enters the person into discipleship to Jesus and into the life of the parish community. Many baptismal fonts today are located as you enter into the back of church to symbolize baptism as the initial sacrament into faith.

Talking to your child

Gather around the baptismal font or pool at your parish before or after Mass sometime. Have everyone dip a hand deeply in the water. Talk about what the water feels like, and what water is good for. Discussion points can include:

- Water is needed by all living things.

- Water is good for cleaning. Baptism in water shows how God washes away our sin and restores us to our best, most beautiful self.

ACTION STEP When watering plants in your garden or in the house, take time to remind your child that water gives life, and that without water nothing could live. Discuss how it is the same with God. And that is why we use water in baptism—to show how God (in and through Jesus) gives us life both here on earth and eternally in heaven.

- Baptism is the first step into our lives as followers of Jesus and the family of God within the Catholic Church.

- The waters of baptism allow us to have a share in the gift of *eternal life* that comes to us through Jesus.

At home, bring out your child's baptismal candle (representing the light of Christ) and white garment (representing one's newness in Christ), along with the photos or video. Share your memories of this sacramental celebration. Explain that even if they don't remember their baptism it was a really important moment and changed them for a lifetime and for eternity.

Consider making it a family faith practice to celebrate the day of your child's baptism. Treat it almost like another birthday. It is one's "birth" into Christian faith, after all. You can light your child's candle and gather to say a family prayer of thanksgiving for the gift of life and the gift of faith. Help your child to understand that we have so much to be grateful for! *Everything* is a gift from God.

Prayer

Heavenly Father, you are the creator of all life. Your greatest gift to the world is Jesus, who offers us, through baptism, the fullness of life. Please continue to pour down your love upon us like the rain. Amen.

Why are there different colors at different times of the year?

For your information

The liturgical calendar contains the seasons and feasts of the Catholic Church year. (Many non-Catholic churches have the same seasons.)

The church year begins on the First Sunday of Advent. Advent is the liturgical season that prepares us for Christmas and the Christmas season. It is important to note that for Catholics, Christmas is not just a day but also a *season*. Christmas, also known as the Solemnity of the Nativity of the Lord, begins on Christmas Eve and continues until the Feast of the Baptism of the Lord in early January. (For a full list of seasons, see the following page.)

Within every season on the liturgical calendar there are various special days. They are, in descending order of importance: *solemnities* (usually relating to Jesus and also Mary), *feasts* (usually for apostles and archangels), *memorials* (for saints). There are several special solemnities, including All Saints and Immaculate Conception of the Blessed Virgin Mary, that are holy days of obligation. This means that Catholics should attend Mass, just like on Sunday.

Talking to your child

A good place to start is to go online and find a Catholic liturgical calendar. Usually these are designed as a wheel or circle. Find the starting point, the First Sunday of Advent, and move clockwise around the calendar with your child.

As you move around the liturgical calendar, note the variety of colors. These are the colors used in liturgies in various ways, most notably in the vestments worn by the priest and deacon in church on

The involvement with your child's relationship to music — from the beginning — will encourage progress and can help strengthen the bond between the two of you.

Later, (*i.e.* after the first year or two), ask the teacher about playing in public. This should include not only playing in studio classes, but for the school class, in church, *etc.* If you have friends over for a meal, have a mini-concert before dinner. *Please* do all this with the blessing and guidance of the teacher, however, for the following reasons:

Playing in public (which means playing for virtually anyone outside the immediate family) can be a pretty unnerving experience for the child. In fact, after recording a dozen CDs, playing hundreds of concerts all over the world and appearing frequently on international radio and television programs — I *still* get slightly nervous when I perform! It's normal to get nervous and anyone who says he doesn't is a fool or a liar.

One of my favorite students in Germany (who was 8 years old at the time) played in his first recital class. After the recital, his mother (an incredible example of an enlightened parent), had this conversation with him,

"How did you feel before the recital?"
"I thought I was going to die."
"How did you feel after the recital?"
"I felt... I felt like I could fly!"

Once a student gets used to performing, he will thrive on it, and the teacher can foster this in a positive comfortable direction. Performing will become "nervously exciting" rather than "nervously threatening."

Stage Parents

I should mention one bizarre aspect of parenting a young musician: *Stage Parents.* This is a pretty uncomfortable subject because there's a fine line between being supportive and being pushy, and you are the only one who is going to be able to find those boundaries.

Yes, you have to push.

No, you can't push too much.

Who said this parental thing was going to be easy...?

By definition, a Stage Parent has decided that little Jimmy or Susie is going to be a great concert artist and the pressure that they put on the child is usually based on unrealistic goals... and it makes everybody miserable.

How many times have you seen parents who stand in the bleachers at little league baseball games, screaming like lunatics if the kid makes an error? I've seen virtually the same thing in music lessons and believe me, it doesn't help matters.

Positive support of the music lessons makes the child (and parent) feel good; being a Stage Parent makes the child (and the parent) feel an unnatural pressure that, ironically, hinders progress. We all want our children to succeed, but that success doesn't necessarily mean that the child will become a great concert artist.

There's a balance here that each parent will have to find based on the child's own personality, goals and ability to handle stress, *but there has to be a balance!*

For me, the balance is achieved by remembering what parenting is about: love, support and encouragement—the things that help a child become his or her own person. I can't imagine a greater joy or honor than helping someone become himself; how could you possibly want less than that for your own child?

Children are no different from adults… OK, they're a little shorter and usually a little messier, but they value the opinion of loved ones just as much and they feel just as deeply as we do—often even more. Push gently but maintain an encouraging attitude. Remember, as important as music lessons are, this isn't brain surgery. There's a balance that only you can find, and if you maintain that balance, your child will learn.

Part of that balance means remembering one of the basic things I described at the beginning: *Music lessons should be a tool that teaches the child to learn.* If you keep that in mind, there won't be a problem.

Remember, there are many things that you can do to help encourage your budding young musician, but the most important thing is simple:

be a parent!

— Chapter Four — The Student

The Child as a Student

For a true beginner, learning an instrument includes much more than simply "learning an instrument." When you really understand what's involved, it's pretty mind-boggling.

To "get-the-finger-at-the-right-place-at-the-right-time," there is the obvious problem of reading music — literally a new language. Then, the visual symbols of the printed music go from the page to the eyes, to the brain, to the nerve paths (which are "mapped" in the brain for recall), to the correct muscles, to (hopefully) the correct place on the instrument... *just to get one note!* All these movements are *extremely* refined and involve millisecond precision and on top of all that, each instrument has its own technical problems that require specialized development. [1]

In spite of this complexity, as crazy as it sounds, one of the most important things that you can do for your young musician is *never let on that it's difficult!*

A child — most of the time — does what he's told and if he's told to do something new, he will assume that the adult who has told him what to do knows that it's possible. A child views an adult that he trusts as an all-knowing, rational creature (ah! if this were always true!).

Why would an adult tell him to do something knowing that it was impossible?! A child assumes that the adult *wants* him to succeed. A child will virtually never question his own ability unless he's *taught* to question it.

Do you realize what a gift that is? As adults, we often question the wrong things and frequently trust no one. Children haven't yet learned these negative traits; as a parent, supporting the music lessons often means taking on the child's innocence. Assume that he *can* and usually he *will!*

---

1. For parents interested in the workings of the brain, muscles, coordination and the acqusition of motor skills when playing music, please consult the book, *How it Works—Why it Works—The Physiology of Playing Music* by Anthony Glise and Dr. Yvonne Delevoye of the Hôpital Université de Strassbourg (France) [in preparation].

In spite of the heavy subject matter, this book is *very* easy to read and offers fascinating insights as to the different physiological aspects facing musicians, based on the most contemporary research in sensorimotor neuroscience. This book is co-written with Dr. Yvonne Delevoye (MD. University Laval, Canada; Ph.D., University of Birmingham, England, *etc.*). A talented violinist herself, Dr. Delevoye is one of the leading scientists in the field and this is the first book to discuss exactly how and why musicians learn, play and practice as we do.

"Mom, I can't play this!"

"Sure you can honey, just try it again a little slower."

The above dialogue will produce better results than the most profound musical analysis and educational theories known to man. Every child can succeed because, frankly, all children are gifted.

As we grow older, we learn to become "un-gifted." We learn to question our innate talents and we learn to bow down to our potential to fail.

Of course there is the occasional Mozart — a *Wunderkind* who defies rational explanation — but the average child is already miraculously gifted until he decides (or more often, is *taught*) that he is not gifted.

Until they learn otherwise, children do not acknowledge a potential for failure. Children don't know these things yet. They assume that they *can! That* is what a gifted child is, *one who is average.* In short, *they're all gifted!*

Pre-instrument Training

While we are slowly catching up in the U.S., the concept of children's music pedagogy is *much* more developed in Europe than in the U.S. The term *pedagogy* means simply *the study of how to teach,* and you'll run across it often in educational materials.

In Europe music pedagogy for children is *highly* developed. There, before children start an instrument, they are often required to take solfège classes. These classes teach rhythms, eye/hand coordination, pitch and interval recognition, note reading, music theory and analysis.

The country most famous for this type of early musical development is France, where a child is required to have several years of solfège before she is permitted to own an instrument! Additionally, by the end of the fourth year of conservatory study, French music students have been exposed to music theory and analysis equal to the first year of U.S. university studies — *usually by the age of 10.*

A cartoon I recently saw in France showed a group of worried French economic advisors sitting around a government office. The caption was, *"Well, our economy may be shot — but the world envies our solfège system!"*

If you are in an area where pre-instrument training is offered, I would *strongly* encourage you to take advantage of it. There are various methods under the names of Suzuki, Yamaha (both of which incorporate work with the instrument), or Kodály, Kindermusik and Orff (which are more "pure" pre-instrument training methods), *etc.*

With even one year of pre-instrument training prior to beginning the instrument, the progress is *at least* twice as fast and twice as easy.

If you're not sure what to do, talk to an instructor at a local college or even the music teacher at your local high school. They will be familiar with these programs, and whether they are offered in your area.

If so, *great* — do it! If not, *great* — there are other options, so don't panic!

If there is no pre-instrument training in your area, simply make sure that the teacher you choose has experience working with children. Most of the contemporary method books for children are heavily influenced by these pre-instrument concepts, so if need be, you can skip pre-instrument training since it's likely that many of these ideas will be built into the method book.

If a child is *very* interested in a specific instrument, it can sometimes be beneficial to begin immediately with that instrument *without* pre-instrument training. A child's innate fascination and love of an instrument (regardless of how illogical and unfounded it may seem to you as the parent) can often override apparent difficulties. This fascination can also push the attention span through the first few months of lessons which are always the most difficult in establishing practice habits, the new relationship with the music teacher, *etc.*

Choosing Which Instrument

So, one way or another (with or without pre-instrument training), you're at the stage when the instrument lessons start. Professional musicians will tell you that specific personalities tend to be more inclined towards specific instruments. For example, someone who is very reserved might do better not playing trumpet, which is very loud and overt.

Guitarists (of which I am one) seem to almost always have facial hair — beard, mustache, *etc.* (naturally I only mean the males...). OK, maybe that's not a good example, but the personality/instrument relationship is truly something to consider.

I would also remind you that the instrument a child chooses to play can have serious *logistic* consequences. For example, if you live in an apartment, drums might not be the best choice. (I have a feeling your neighbors would rapidly agree!)

A friend of mine who plays with the French National Orchestra had a child in this phase of choosing an instrument. He called me at my home in Germany and said with a depressed and exasperated voice, *"Naomi* (his daughter) *"...knows what she wants to play..."* [long, pregnant pause] "...the ***HARP!"***

My eyes rolled back in my head, my body quivered and I gave an appropriate gasp of empathetic terror!

By way of an explanation... harps are *insanely* expensive, and among other serious logistics, *often* require buying a new car that is large enough to haul the beast around, not to mention rearranging furniture to fit it in the house, *etc.*

Nevertheless, most children seem to have a sixth sense in choosing an instrument that best suits their personality. Let your child make that decision and trust the good judgment that he has learned from you. It may not be *your* choice, but it will almost always be the *correct* choice. Just remember that with some instruments there are *serious* logistics which you should carefully consider!

If you haven't yet bought an instrument, *let the teacher help!* The teacher will have a better understanding of how to find an acceptable instrument that's in your price range and sometimes (less in the U.S. than in Europe) a teacher will get a professional discount from the music store which can decrease your price by up to 10%.

Many teachers I know use this visit to a music store as the first lesson. Keep in mind that for the music teacher, choosing an instrument is *work* and takes a great deal of time. Don't assume that the teacher is going to do this for fun on his free time. Musicians love music, but just about the *last* thing that a musician wants to do with his spare time is hang around in a music store! Honestly, do you go to work on your day off...?

Practice Time

Once your child has chosen an instrument and is actually taking lessons, the first battle you're going to have — usually within the first month — is over practicing. A simple solution that you can initiate before this problem comes up is a "contract." This doesn't have to be a legal document that permits you to drag your eight-year old in front of a magistrate to threaten her with incarceration, but...

A contract can consist of any number of things, depending on the age of the student (all of which are essentially "bribes"). A contract can be as simple as awarding a cookie after practicing, dessert after dinner, *etc.* It might include permission to use the family car one evening a week (though I wouldn't suggest this for your eight-year old). Anything is possible, so be creative, but work on the terms together and write it out; both of you sign it — *and stick to the contract or it will have no effect!*

The amount of practice time will be set by the teacher and will obviously vary with the age of the student, but in the beginning you're usually not looking at much more than 30 minutes per day.

Even with this short period, it can be a good idea to set a timer (kept in another room so the ticking doesn't distract your child) and half-way through, take a 5-minute break. Then at the end of the practice session, have some sort of prize, such as cookies, soda, *etc.*

I know some parents who also set the timer for the break — otherwise the child may "forget" to go back and finish the practice session. Hey, we all have moments of selective memory!

After the first year, the practice time should usually be pushed up to an hour per day (but still including a break). It is critical that the practice time is *focused; i.e.,* no TV or radio in the background. [2] Just as important, it should be "intelligent practice," *not* just playing though pieces. I'll discuss this further in the next chapter.

The role that your child is assuming as a music student *doesn't* have to mean that she will become a concert musician. It *does* mean that she will develop an element of her personality through the instrument that would otherwise lie dormant her entire life.

We all want the best for our children. Encourage this aspect. *It will be worth it!*

---

2. Remember you mother complaining, "...Don't do your homework with the radio on!"? Well, sorry, but current research proves she was right — and it's just as important when practicing an instrument! For more details, see *How it Works—Why it Works—The Physiology of Playing Music* by Anthony Glise and Dr. Yvonne Delevoye of the Hôpital Université de Strassbourg (France) [in preparation], *op. cit.*

— Chapter Five — Practicing

How your child practices and *how consistently* he practices — not necessarily *how long* he practices — is going to determine his degree of progress. Teachers usually explain all this in the lesson, but it often simply doesn't stick. The student gets home, starts practicing incorrectly and you may never know it.

You are the one who will have to make sure he sits down to practice and monitor practice time to insure that the work is constructive.

Practice Schedule

The practice session should be scheduled for a specific time of day. This doesn't have to be the same time each day; with all the activities a child has, this is often impossible, but it has to be *every* day.

It can help to have a weekly calendar. Write in everything from breakfast to bed-time, and obviously include the practice time. If the child can maintain this type of organization of his time for one year, it will become habit —and frankly, a habit that will make his entire life run more smoothly. If this looks like it may be a problem, as I mentioned before, a contract between the two of you is usually the easiest solution.

Below is a rough diagram of an effective practice schedule.

Fig. 1. Diagram of Effective Practice Time for a Beginner

- Warm-ups (5 min.)
- Listen to cassette tape of the assigned piece (5 min.)
- Isolated practice (on the new piece) (10 min.)
- Break (games) (not counted in total time)
- Run (playing through old pieces, *etc.*) This is "fun time." (10 min.)

Within the first year or so, the basic rhythms and notes are learned. At this point, the "game time" at the break can usually be dropped. However, clapping (and/or) singing rhythms is very advantageous and should still be practiced.

Below is a rough diagram of practice time for a student in this secondary phase. Note that this one has the same basic design as in figure 1, but as I'll explain later, the goals are much more advanced.

Fig. 2. Diagram of Effective Practice Time after about 1 Year.[3]

- Warm-ups (10 min.)
- Listen to cassette tape of the assigned piece (10 min.)
- Isolated practice (on the new piece) (20 min.)
- Break (not counted in total time)
- Run (playing through old pieces, *etc.*) This is "fun time." (20 min.)

Ironically when practice time is very structured, the student will practice *more* than expected. This is especially true during the last phase of a practice session when the student is "running pieces." At this point, because he can play basically anything he wants, it's simply more fun and this stage will often extend long beyond the suggested duration. This is often the most productive time, since it is a direct application and review of different technical and musical ideas found in the pieces.

Because each stage of the practice time involves such specific activities, I'll discuss them separately.

---

3. I am using the concept of "one year" in a *very* loose manner. Older students may reach this second level after only a few months, while a very young child might not arrive there for several years. Don't panic if your child is going more slowly than these diagrams indicate. If you're concerned about progress, talk to the teacher.

Warm-ups

Let me first remind you that the correct sitting or standing position while practicing is critical for any instrument. Not only does this position arrange the hands, feet, *etc.* to make the correct movements more easily, but a good playing position will also help keep the chest cavity erect so that breathing is more free. For singers, this is obviously necessary, but for instrumentalists it is just as important.

When we play, the oxygen not only feeds the brain but also helps maintain a steady blood-flow to the extremities. All this helps keep the hands warm which means they stay more relaxed.

Physical tension (which is often a result of a bad playing position) not only makes certain movements difficult, but can result in over-straining muscles and tendons, all of which can cause physical damage.

At the beginning of the practice session, it is *essential* that the student does at least 5 minutes of warm-ups. These should be prescribed by the teacher since each instrument (and each student in various levels) will have different needs. *Under no circumstances should the warm-ups ever be skipped!*

In fact, sometimes I have students who *honestly* don't have the time to practice one or two days per week. On these days, I require them to do *only* the warm-ups.

This type of severe scheduling problem is particularly common in Europe, where the hours of the school day are often irregular (even in elementary school). One day a student may have no afternoon classes and the next day she may go from 8 a.m. to 6 p.m. with only a twenty minute lunch break.

Listening to the Recording

After the warm-ups, or perhaps before the practice session, listen to the recording of the assigned piece. I can't begin to tell you how important this is!

Many methods come with a recording of all the pieces in the method book. If yours didn't, bring a cassette to the lesson and ask the teacher to make a tape of the pieces.

If the student can hear the piece he is working on with precise rhythms, notes, tempo and for more advanced students dynamics, articulation and phrasing it can save hours of incorrect practice.

Ironically, this is the one element of practicing that parents usually let slide, while this is one of the most important — even on the days that a student can't practice on the instrument.

Listening to the tape can be incorporated into the practice time (as shown in figures 1 and 2) or done during the break, while playing the games, eating dinner, or running errands in the car — anywhere. *Please* don't let this slide! In all honesty, it can double the rate of progress.

If the teacher records all the pieces in the method book, *listen to the entire tape* — even as background music during some other activity. This will insure that the child recognizes each new piece and again, the learning process is *radically* accelerated!

Games

Particularly for younger children, there are hundreds of games that can be played to learn and reinforce different aspects of music. Your teacher will know which books you should buy and will suggest which games will help the most.

Some of the most popular games, are:

• *Flash cards*. Much like those you probably used in school to learn multiplication tables, a deck of flash cards can be a tremendous help. The notes or rhythms that are being learned in the lesson are written on index cards; the parent says *"Where is the quarter note?"* or *"Where is the note 'E'?"* and the child picks it out of a half dozen or so cards laid face-up on a table. Below are examples of cards for rhythmic practice and note practice.

Fig. 3. Sample Rhythm Cards.

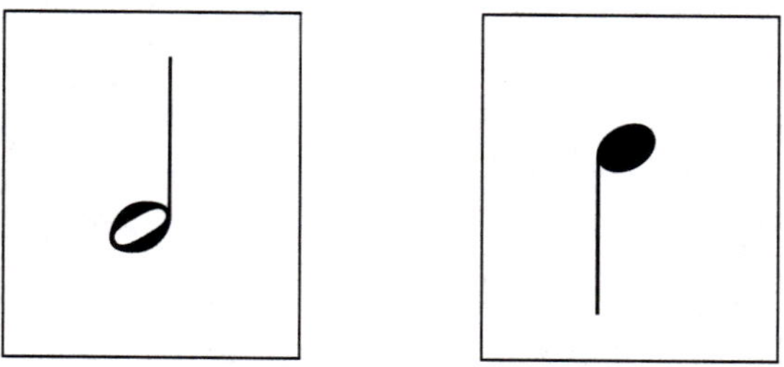

Fig. 4. Sample Note Cards.

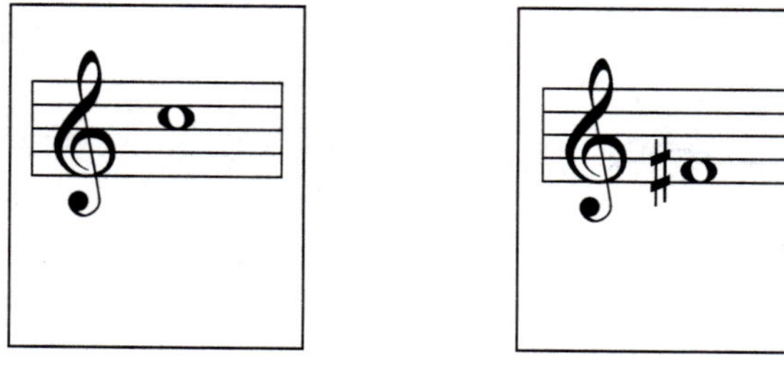

You can make these cards at home and play the game during the break. Simply add a new card each time the student learns a new note, rhythm, *etc.* Remember that you can write the answers (the name of the rhythm, note, *etc.*) on the back of the card if you're not familiar with music yourself.

The rhythm flash cards can also be laid side-by-side to make up more complex rhythms. Likewise, the different note cards can be laid side-by-side to make up different melodies which, in-turn, can be played on the instrument.

• *Words for Rhythms.* This is an easy and effective way to teach specific rhythms. With any new rhythmic combination, find a spoken phrase or word that matches it. This can also be combined with the flash cards. For example, the rhythm below might be "spoken" as: *"I go walking fast!"* (long—long—short, short, long—).

Virtually any spoken phrases are possible as long as they precisely match the rhythm. Be sure to use characters from the child's favorite stories or TV characters, *etc.*

An old friend, Eve Weiss, a brilliant guitarist/music pedagogue in New York City, is obsessed with *The Wizard of Oz.* For her and her child Jonathan, using the words "Dorothy," or "Toto," *etc.*, make this type of game more personalized and more fun.

• *Staff Games.* Learning notes on the staff can be confusing. One physically-active game is to stick five lines of tape on the floor to represent the musical staff. When you say the name of a note, the child jumps to that line or space.

You can also throw beanbags onto the staff and have the child say the names of the notes where the beanbags land, and even write out these random notes on staff paper and play them on the instrument. In doing this, the student can compose his own small piece of music.

These more physically-oriented games can be fantastic for younger students to play during the break because it gives them a chance to move around a bit and can release the nervous energy that often builds during concentrated practice.

To list all such musical games — and those you might invent yourself — is impossible. There are hundreds of books out there. It's worth a little research because the games will help reinforce note and rhythmic development more than anything else — and frankly — they're fun!

Obviously, finding and playing games that are applicable to the pieces being learned means you must be in touch with the teacher every week. Particularly for younger students these games can be unbelievably productive, but there *must* be a direct connection between the games and the student's weekly assignment.

More than anything else, the *quality* and *consistency* of the practice time will directly determine progress. It's an element of musical study that is exclusively *your* responsibility to monitor at home with the same sense of concern and conviction as you would any other endeavor that your child pursues.

— Chapter Six —
Practice Techniques

Beginner's Techniques

Now down to business — *how* to practice. As I said before, the teacher has probably explained practice techniques in the lesson, but you need to know how practicing should work in order to monitor it at home. Remember that a teacher sees the student only a short time each week. The rest of the time (*i.e.* when practicing at home) *you* need to keep the practice time structured.

In general, there are two types of practicing: *practicing* and *practicing for performance.*

• ***Practicing for performance*** occurs when a piece is already totally learned and you simply play through it from beginning to end to prepare it for a lesson or recital. The goal is to create a sense of flow throughout the piece. If the student stops, it is by *choice* rather than *necessity* due to an error. *When* the player stops, it is only to fix minor problems or to try different interpretive ideas. This is what most students are doing when they *think* they are practicing.

• ***Practicing,*** on the other hand, is *work* and is probably best defined by one simple word: *isolation.*

To explain this a little better, let me tell you a story. Often in my masterclasses for upper-level students and professional musicians, when they make a mistake, I stop them and ask what happened. Invariably, they give me a bewildered look and say,

"I played the wrong note!"

"No!" I respond, *"How is that possible? All the right notes are already on the instrument! It's impossible to play a 'wrong note.'— You made a wrong* movement *that* resulted *in the wrong note!"*

A little esoteric, but true. In learning an instrument we are learning *movements.* Some of these are highly refined and virtually all these movements require isolated training. That's what real practicing is about.

There are several ways to "practice" as opposed to "practicing performing." One of the most popular techniques is "running" a piece. Here, a student plays until there is a problem, he then stops, and plays over the area several times, from before the problem to slightly after the problem. When the problem area feels secure, he continues until the next problem spot arises and then repeats the same process.

This approach works well for more advanced players, but it assumes that the student can already read music well and already has most of the movements consciously learned (*cf.* figure 5).

Fig. 5. "Running" a Piece for Practice. (Numbers show the sequence of events.)

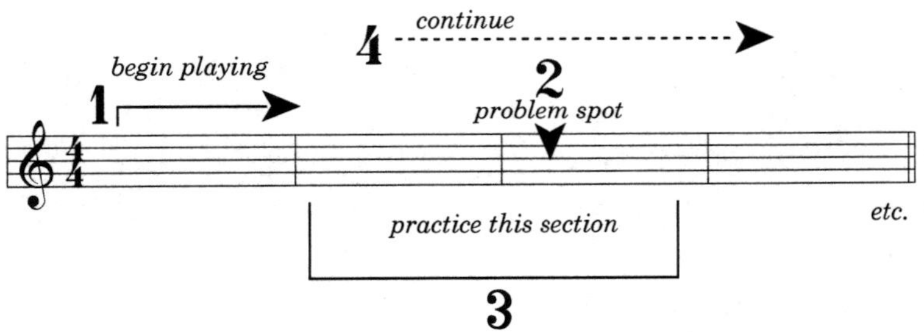

Another approach is the "overlap method of practicing." It is highly effective and frankly, most professionals I know use this following method.

In overlap practicing, one or two measures are played several times in a row. Then the next section is played and the two sections are grouped together and played several times. Then the following section is played several times and grouped with the previous, and so on.

The advantages to this method are *tremendous*. First, *nothing* is taken for granted. Every section is isolated, then linked to the previous *and* the following section. Also, no time is wasted playing sections that have already been learned while unstable sections are skipped over (*cf.* figure 6).

Fig. 6. "Overlap" Method of Practicing. (Numbers show sequence of events.)

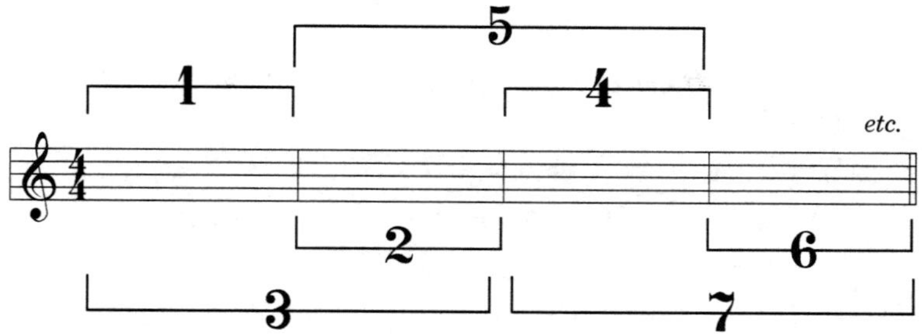

I would *strongly* encourage using the overlap technique when practicing. It's fast, effective and leaves *very* little room for error. It also breaks the piece into manageable sections that will make even the longest composition seem less intimidating to the student.

Once the student can play a piece using the overlap method, not only is it learned but the piece has usually been memorized at the same time — almost by accident!

At that point, he should start running the piece, playing from beginning to end. If any mistakes occur at this stage, they should be isolated and played several times correctly. Then he continues playing through the piece. If a student has trouble memorizing, using the overlap method is almost always the solution.

A passing note: this may seem obvious, but I want to point out that in the practicing phase, *a piece needs to be played slowly!* Then, over a week or so, the tempo is gradually increased. Often a student thinks that if he can't hear a mistake, there isn't one. Thus, his solution to not hearing mistakes is to play so quickly that he can't hear the errors!

This approach is terrifyingly wrong! As strange as it sounds, there is no difference between playing quickly and playing slowly. Playing quickly is simply less slow — *the movements are all still the same.*

Playing slowly lets the student hear any mistakes and correct them. It also insures that the movements are intentional so they are consciously learned and mapped by the brain for recall, not simply executed by chance. [2]

Usually, if a piece has more than three mistakes that require the student to stop, it is too early to start running the piece and he should go back and use the overlap method.

Intermediate Techniques [4]

After the initial year or so, the practice techniques remain the same, but the *goal* of practicing changes slightly. Obviously, the correct notes, rhythms and overall tempo of the piece are still critical, but there are additional aspects that enter into the study.

With most instruments, the timbre (tone color), articulation and phrasing become more and more important in the intermediate phase. These are what give a piece an individual interpretation.

While these are more advanced techniques, the teacher will usually include these elements on the recording from the very beginning. This makes them less foreign when they are introduced to the student.

---

4. Various practice techniques for advanced musicians are discussed in the university textbook: Glise, A. *Classical Guitar Pedagogy — A Handbook for Teachers.* Pacific: Mel Bay Publications, 1997.

While many of the ideas in this book are much too advanced for a beginner, it would be worth checking it out of your local library. This will give you an idea of what's in-store for the future as your young musician progresses.

There are hundreds of intermediate practice techniques that encourage technical development and help solve specific problems. The most basic include:

• *Dot rhythms.* When a specific phrase sounds uneven or certain notes are insecure, dotting the rhythm — in both directions — can solve the problem.

What this means is, for example, if the original melody has an even rhythm (as if you were walking — *right, left, right, left*), it should be practiced unevenly — or "dotted." Thus, it would sound as if, rather than walking evenly, you were skipping — *long, short, long, short* (or reversed- *short, long, short long*).

For example in figure 7, the original passage could be practiced as in figure 8.

Fig. 7. Original Passage.

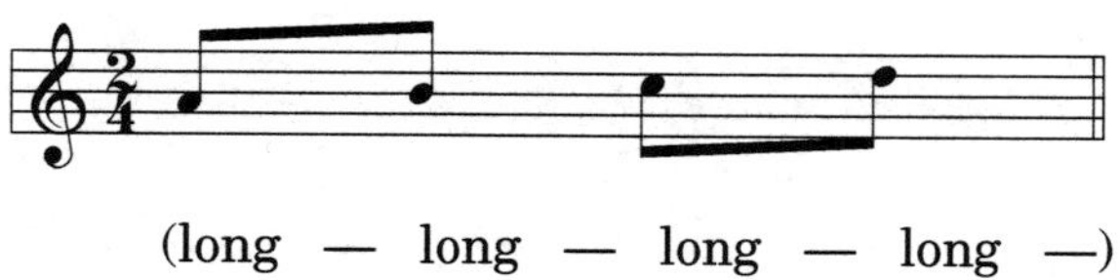

Fig. 8. Passage Dotted for Practice.

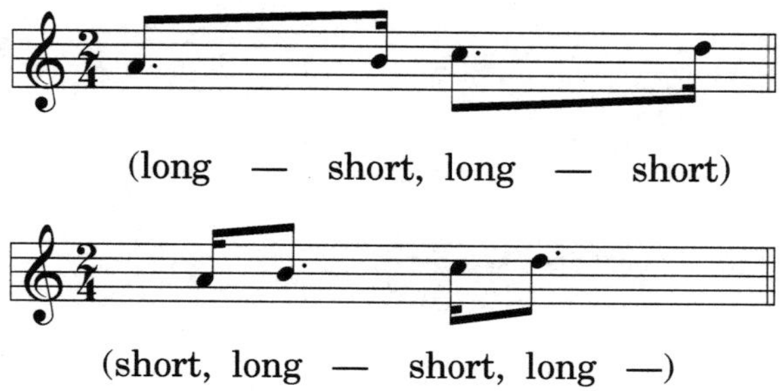

By dotting rhythms, the fingers are forced to react more quickly and precisely between each note; then, when the piece is played with its normal rhythm, the instability is usually solved.

• *Playing hands separately.* This obviously works only for instruments where both hands are used. The student simply practices one hand separately without the other, then *vice versa.*

This can quickly stabilize complicated movements between hands by isolating the movements into more concise, manageable problems.

• *Targeting notes.* This approach is similar to speaking a sentence and stopping on each word in order to practice the enunciation. In musical practice, this helps when a phrase or passage is very quick, or has a new or uncomfortable movement from one note to another.

In this technique, the phrase is played and then the student stops on the second note, then he begins again and stops on the third, then the fourth, *etc.*

This approach isolates specific movements, and causes an accent or emphasis on each note individually, which ensures that each note and each movement to each note is secure.

Fig. 9. Original Passage.

Fig. 10. Passage Practiced to Target Each Note.

At the more advanced stages, a student will encounter an infinite number of small challenges and each one will require a specific practice technique. The teacher will help design these practice techniques and as long as you stay in touch with the teacher, you will know what *should* be happening in the practice time at home.

Practicing doesn't have to be unpleasant work. In fact, if practicing is approached methodically (using the practice methods described above) the sense of immediate accomplishment is *extremely* high, the work is more fun and the student will make more progress.

A Word of Encouragement

You WILL survive your kid taking music lessons! I promise!

As I said in the beginning, it's just going to take a little patience, a little work and occasionally a few cotton balls stuffed in your ears! Nonetheless, you'll be fine.

Probably the most important thing that you can do is something you do already: *act out of love.* If you have children, you know that they can sometimes be a little difficult (an understatement...?).

Music lessons can complicate that situation. Musical study can become grounds for new battles, *but only if you let it.* On the other hand, music lessons can be a tremendous bonding experience between you and your child—a bond that can last a lifetime.

Maintain a sense of humor, and *constantly* act out of love. Keep in mind that your child is learning something that — from day one — is going to be a tremendous asset to him for the rest of his life. Patience will often be your greatest contribution to this learning process.

Act out of love and remember that you'll look back on this time as something exciting, rewarding and (as unbelievable as it seems) in 20 years you'll actually *miss* hearing the sound of the instrument screaming away in the next room!

With my very best wishes
for you and your young musician,

Anthony L. GLISE

Glossary for the Musically-Challenged Parent

I realize that some of you may feel as though you're getting in a little over your heads. It will be fine! If you're totally unfamiliar with musical terminology, however, this small glossary will help.

I have included words that might arise in the beginning lessons as well as those you might need in buying an instrument.

Many words are so logical I have simply avoided them. For example, a *gear* (on the tuning key of a guitar) is simply a "gear" and needs no explanation. Some words could be confusing, however. A *frog* does not mean the little green animal your 8-year old hid in his pocket during church last week; a *time change* has nothing to do with Daylight-Savings Time and a *piano reduction* is not a scientific process to make your piano smaller so it fits in the living room. These are all harmless words that you'll find creeping slowly into your vocabulary as your child continues his or her musical studies.

I strongly encourage you to buy a comprehensive music dictionary in the near future. If you have a computer at home, how many computer books do you have lying around? Music has just as many specialized words so you should buy a good dictionary, but for the first year or so, this condensed glossary will easily get you through! [1]

---

1. The dictionary used by most professional musicians is the *Harvard Dictionary of Music* (in various editions, published by Harvard University Press). It is very affordable (even in hardback), is the "industry standard" and can be found in virtually any bookstore.

— A —

a cappella Singing a cappella simply means singing without any *accompaniment (q.v).* This is a common style in *sacred music (q.v.).*

accent If a composer wants a specific note or chord played louder or "heavier" than the surrounding notes, he indicates this by placing an accent sign above or below the note which should be accented. An example of accents is given below.

Fig. 1. Example of written accents.

accidental All *sharps* or *flats (q.v.)* are usually indicated by the composer in the *key signature (q.v.)* at the beginning of each line in the music. Sometimes, however, he might decide to change one of these notes, so he'll put a sharp, flat or natural sign directly before that single note. That will alter the note for the entire measure.

At the end of the measure, the note reverts back to the original pitch the composer indicated in the key signature (unless he changes it again later).

accompaniment The accompaniment is the part of music that serves as the "background" for another more important part.

accompany To accompany someone in music means to play the background part of the music while they play the main part.

acoustic An acoustic instrument is one that uses no electricity or battery to produce its sound.

acoustics This refers to the way music sounds in a specific room, concert hall, *etc.* Some rooms will be more "live" (*i.e.* they have more echo), while some will be more "dead" or "dry" (have less echo).

action The action is the feeling of how easy or difficult the keys are to press on a piano, organ, *etc.* With stringed instruments, the action refers to how high (far away) or low (near) the strings are to the *fingerboard (q.v.).* Always check the action when buying a new or used instrument.

ad libitum This means "at your leisure" and refers to a passage in music where the player may alter the *tempo (q.v.)* as he likes. He may play more slowly, more quickly, *etc.*

æsthetics In ancient Greek philosophy, æsthetics meant simply "beauty." In music, the term is used to refer to the study of something beautiful. Something may be "æsthetically pleasing," *etc.*

aleatoric music This is a style of music, like film music or rock music. Aleatoric music is written by the composer so that there is some element of chance in the performance. For example, he may compose a specific passage of notes, then write a section where those same notes may be played as many times as the performer wishes before he continues playing. An entire piece may be composed in an aleatoric style. This music has been popular only since *ca.* 1945 and although it is a fairly complex style, some composers have written aleatoric music for students.

alla breve This is a rather antiquated way to refer to the *time signature (q.v.)* 2/2 (indicated by a "C" with a slash through it). Both this and our time signature sign for *common time (q.v.)* stem from the Middle Ages. Both are still sometimes used today.

Fig. 2. Example of *alla breve* time signature.

alteration (chromatic alteration) —*cf. chromatic*

alto —*cf. voice*

anacrusis Also called an *upbeat*, or *pick-up*, occurs when a piece begins with only a partial measure. It's basically the same as beginning a word with an unaccented syllable. *Ex.* The word "everyone" has the accent on the first syllable. The word "computer" has the accent on the second syllable.

In music, however, because the beginning of each measure is *always* strong, if you have a piece that starts with a weak beat, it *can't* start at the beginning of a measure. Thus, at the very beginning of the piece, it starts (part-way) through a measure (on a weak beat). That partial measure at the beginning of a piece is an *anacrusis.*

Fig. 3. Beginning of a Piece Without an Anacrusis.

Fig. 4. Beginning of a Piece With an Anacrusis.

analysis Musical analysis involves the study of the way a piece has been composed, the way the different *chords (q.v.)* move from one to the other, the way the *melody (q.v.)* is written, and the way the sections of the piece fit together, *etc.* A teacher will teach basic aspects of analysis to a student because if a musician understands how a piece is constructed, it can make the piece easier to learn.

answer *—cf. antecedent*

antecedent Two *phrases (q.v.) together* are often composed to sound like a "question and answer." The first phrase (the question) is called an *antecedent* and the second phrase (the answer) is called the *consequent (q.v.).* It's important for a student to understand where these phrases are in order to perform them with the correct interpretation.

appoggiatura *—cf. grace note*

arpeggiate When you arpeggiate, you play the different notes of a chord separately rather than together. Arpeggiation is used frequently in *accompaniment (q.v.).* The word *arpeggiate* is used to imply playing a chord or series of chords, while the word *broken (q.v.)* is usually said in reference to merely a few notes, such as a chord or a series of chords. Both terms imply the same general execution on the instrument: playing the lowest note first, followed immediately by the remaining notes.

arpeggio An arpeggio is what you get when you arpeggiate a chord, *etc. Arpeggios* and *scales (q.v.)* are often used as *warm-ups (q.v.).*

arrangement An arrangement usually means a piece that was written for one instrument and rewritten, or "arranged" for another. *Cf.* also *transcription.*

articulation This is similar to when you emphasize or de-emphasize different words or syllables when speaking. There are various signs to specify different types of articulations. Articulation is often indicated by the composer but can be added by the player at his own discretion, which helps create a more interesting and personalized interpretation. *Cf. Appendix 5 — Sample Staff Layout* for an example.

augmented A note (usually in a chord) is said to be augmented when one of the notes is raised one-half step further than is normal in a key. An *interval (q.v.)* may be augmented if it is raised one-half step further than normal in a key. *Cf.* also *diminished.*

autograph manuscript *—cf. manuscript*

— B —

1 **bar** —*cf. measure*

2 **bar** (bar chord) A bar or bar chord in playing the guitar, lute, banjo, *etc.,* is a technique whereby the first finger is laid flat across the *fingerboard (q.v.)* to depress more than one string.

3 **bar line** The music is divided up into small sections called *measures* (*q.v.*). Think of them as words in a sentence. These small sections (or "measures") are divided by a vertical line that is drawn through the staff and the area between these lines is a measure.

N.B. It has simply become tradition to say "bar line" even though it should logically be called a "measure line." *Cf. Appendix 5 — Sample Staff Layout* for an example.

baritone —*cf. voice*

1 **bass** —*cf. voice*

2 **bass bar** A bass bar is a long, flat, thin piece of wood inside a violin, viola, cello or bass which is glued lengthwise underneath the *soundboard (q.v.).* This is one of the most important parts inside these instruments. Where it is placed is a virtual science and will drastically alter the sound of an instrument. In buying an instrument, always have the teacher or a repairman check to make sure the *soundpost (q.v.)* and the bass bar are secure since a loose soundpost or bass bar can make even a fantastic instrument sound terrible.

beam Sometimes two or more consecutive notes (which would normally have a *flag (q.v.)* to indicate duration) will be grouped together by a beam rather than two or more separate flags. *Cf. Appendix 2 — Rhythms* for an example. *Cf.* also *flag.*

beat Imagine walking — right, left, right, left, *etc.* These are beats. A beat is usually a steady "pulse" within a piece but it can be divided, shortened or elongated. *Cf.* also *dotted.*

bell A bell on a trumpet, trombone, French Horn, *etc,* is the end shaped like a funnel where the sound comes out.

body On a stringed instrument, the body is the larger part below the *neck (q.v.).*

bout Looking at a guitar from the front (where the strings are) the widest part of the *body (q.v.)* at the bottom is the *lower bout;* the narrowest part (about where the soundhole is) is the *middle bout;* the highest part — where the *neck (q.v.)* attaches — is the *upper bout.* All instruments with this basic shape (guitar, violin, viola, cello, *etc.*) have an upper, middle and lower bout. This is important in buying an instrument, because the size of the bouts should be correct for a student or the instrument won't be comfortable.

1 **brace** The braces in an instrument are the long thin pieces of wood glued inside the *soundbox (q.v.)* of the instrument. Strictly speaking, a brace is glued directly across (in various patterns) the back and the *table (q.v.),* while a *rib (q.v.)* is along the edges of the back and sides and the sides and the *table (q.v.).* A brace does two important things:

1) it helps support the construction of the instrument, *and,*
2) it helps conduct the sound through the *soundbox (q.v.),*
all of which can drastically effect the sound of an instrument.

There are many different bracing designs for different instruments. These designs (and even the shape of the braces and the wood that is used) can have a *tremendous* influence on the sound of an instrument. In buying an instrument, be sure to have the teacher or music store salesperson explain the bracing system of the specific instrument you are considering buying. *Cf.* also *rib.*

2 **brace** A brace in written music is the wavy line at the beginning of two or more staffs of music which connect them. *Cf. Appendix 5—Sample Staff Layout* for an example.

1 **breath marking** *—cf. comma*

2 **breath support** When you play any instrument that requires that you breathe (singing, flute, saxophone, *etc.*) the breath support means having the correct posture so the breathing is comfortable and steady.

bridge The bridge of a string instrument is where the strings are either connected at the lower *bout (q.v.),* or where they are raised (by the bridge) above the *fingerboard (q.v.)* at the lower bout. When buying an instrument always check around the bridge for any warping of the wood, since this is an area of the instrument with a great deal of stress from the tension of the strings. *Cf.* also *nut,* which does the same thing (raising the strings above the fingerboard), but the nut is on the other end of the strings at the *head (q.v.)* of the instrument where you tune.

broken Two or more notes are played broken when you play them separately instead of together. *Broken* is usually used to mean several notes, while the word *arpeggiate* is usually said in reference to playing more notes, such as a chord or series of chords. Both terms imply the same general execution on the instrument: playing the lowest note first, followed immediately by the remaining notes.
Cf. also *arpeggiate.*

builder A builder is a person who makes large instruments (organ, piano, *etc.*). A *luthier (q.v.)* builds smaller instruments.

— C —

cadence At the end of a phrase, section or an entire piece, a composer will usually write a specific order of chords so the piece sounds finished. The best-known cadence is the *chord progression (q.v.)* that you hear in a church hymn when you sing the final "Amen." There are many different types of cadences.

cane This is the bamboo-like material used to make a *reed (q.v.)* for a clarinet, oboe, *etc.*

capo A capo is a device that clamps on the neck of a guitar or lute, pressing all the strings to shorten the vibrating length of the strings. This permits the guitarist to play *chords (q.v.)* so they sound higher, which can make it easier to sing some songs. A capo is usually not used by classical guitarists, since they will simply play using a *bar chord (q.v.).*

cautionary accidental An *accidental (q.v.)* is a *sharp, flat* or *natural sign (q.v.)* that is not in the normal *key signature (q.v.)* (at the beginning of each line of music). It alters that specific note for the entire measure.

However sometimes a composer wants to make sure that the player remembers (especially if the note happens again in the same measure), so he'll write the same sharp, flat or natural sign (usually in parenthesis) just to remind the player that it should *still* be sharp, flat or natural. This is a cautionary accidental.

Since an accidental is only for one measure (when you go to the next measure, the note returns to it's original pitch in the key signature), a composer will also sometimes add a cautionary accidental to remind the player that this note should still be altered.

chamber music This is any music written for a small group of musicians. In size, it's between solo (for one person) and orchestral (for an orchestra). If your child is in a pooling group with three or more players, the teacher will probably refer to the piece they're playing together as "chamber music."

chance music *—cf. aleatoric music*

chord A chord is usually three or more *notes (q.v.)* that sound correct together. On a plucked string instrument, a chord can also mean a specific left hand form, whereby the player holds down several notes at the same time. This is different for bowed instruments (violin, *etc.*). For these instruments (although they are also playing a chord), it is called a *double stop, triple stop* or *quadruple stop,* depending on how many notes are written. *Cf.* also *double stop.*

chord progression This is a series of *chords (q.v.),* one after another, in a specific order. Often (especially in popular music) the same chord progression will be repeated over and over.

1 **chromatic** Used as an adjective, chromatic indicates any note that has been altered to be higher or lower, indicated by a *sharp, flat* or *natural sign (q.v.).*

2 **chromatic** Chromatic can be used as a noun defining a type of *scale (q.v.),* exercise, *etc.* It means that a musical element doesn't fit into a specific *key (q.v.). Cf.* also *diatonic.*

clef This is the strange-looking design at the beginning of each staff. There are a dozen or so of these that give the musician a reference point for where the notes are, but an instrument will usually only use one or two clefs specific to that instrument. *Cf. Appendix 5— Sample Staff Layout* for an example. Some of the different clefs look like:

𝄞 𝄠 𝄢 𝄣 𝄡

climax This is the highest (and often the most important and the loudest) part of a *phrase (q.v.).* The climax frequently occurs between the *antecedent* and *consequent (q.v.)* phrases.

coda This is the very last section of a piece. The sign for a coda is: 𝄌. *Cf. Appendix 1 — Various Signs in Music* for a detailed explanation.

color *—cf. timbre*

comma A comma is a written sign in the music that tells a player or singer when to breathe. Commas are very important since they help the player divide *phrases (q.v.)* into sections that sound logical and makes them easier to play. The sign for a comma is: , .

common time This is a rather antiquated way to refer to the *time signature (q.v.)* 4/4 (indicated by a "C"). Both this and our time signature sign for *alla breve (q.v.)* stem from the Middle Ages. Both are still sometimes used today.

Fig. 5. Example of *common time* time signature.

concert pitch One pitch sounds different from another because of the number of vibrations per second. If there are more vibrations, the pitch sounds higher. If there are fewer, it sounds lower. This used to make it difficult to know how you should tune an instrument because there were no real rules for the number of vibrations per second of each note.

Finally, in the 20th-Century, the International Bureau of Weights and Measures decided that the pitch A should be 440 cycles per second and all the other notes are tuned in relation to that pitch. This is now the standard rule used by most musicians to tune their instruments and is referred to as "concert pitch."

concerto This is a composition for orchestra and a solo musician. A double concerto is for two soloists with orchestra, a triple concerto is for three soloists with orchestra, *etc.*

consequent Two phrases together are often composed to sound like a "question and answer." The first phrase (the question) is called an *antecedent (q.v.)* and the second phrase (the answer) is called the *consequent*. It's important for a student to understand where these phrases are in order to perform them with the correct interpretation.

conservatory A conservatory is a university-level school that focuses on the performing arts (music, theater, dance, *etc.*). Some conservatories have an "extension" or continuing education department where younger students and adults may study.

consonant Two or more pitches (or even an entire piece) that sound pleasant when played together are "consonant." This is obviously a very subjective concept. It is the opposite of *dissonant (q.v.)*.

contrary motion Two melodies played together can move in relation to each other in three different ways: *contrary* (in totally opposite directions), *oblique* (in basically the same direction, but not the same distance) and *parallel* (in exactly the same direction and distance). *Cf.* figures 6-8 below.

Fig. 6. Contrary motion between two lines.

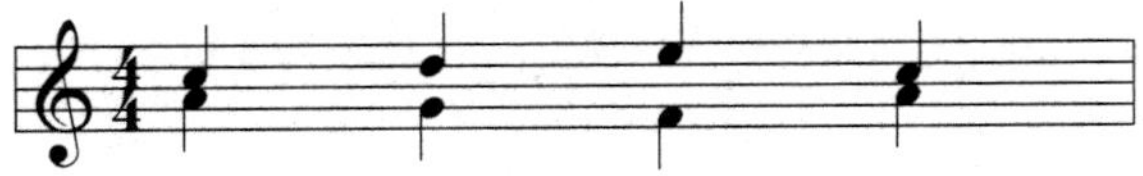

Fig. 7. Oblique motion between two lines.

Fig. 8. Parallel motion between two lines.

[1] **cork** This is the material (actually made of cork) on the inner part of joints of many woodwind instruments used to insure an air-tight seal between two sections of an instrument .

[2] **cork grease** This is a type of fat that is smeared on the cork to help slide the joints of a woodwind instrument on or off more easily.

counterpoint This is a style of composition whereby a *subject (q.v.)* or "melody" is played on top of itself or below itself to create the *harmony (q.v.)* (as opposed to having the harmony as chords and the melody over the top, as in a normal song that one would sing). There are many styles of counterpoint and many specific ways to create a composition using this compositional technique.

One specific type of composition that uses counterpoint is called a *fugue (q.v.)*.

crescendo To crescendo means to gradually play louder and louder A crescendo is often indicated by the composer but can be added by the player at his own discretion which helps create a more interesting and personalized interpretation. *Cf. Appendix 5— Sample Staff Layout* for an example. *Cf.* also *decrescendo.*

cross fingering Cross fingering is a term used almost exclusively in keyboard playing. If you tap your fingers, one after another, on a table, the fingers are in order. However, if you reach one finger over another (breaking the pattern of the normal positions of the fingers), this would be similar to as a cross fingering on a keyboard. These are sometimes necessary to extend a continuous melody or scale on the instrument.

cue A cue is usually a hand sign given by a conductor or a leader of a musical ensemble to tell a player when to make an *entrance(q.v.). Cf.* also *downbeat.*

1 **cut** *—cf. dampen*

2 **cut off** This is a *cue (q.v.)* from a conductor to tell a player to stop playing.

3 **cut time** *—cf. alla breve*

— D —

da capo (D.C.) This phrase (which means "to the head" in Italian) is usually abbreviated *D.C.* It tells the player to jump back to the beginning of the piece and play from there again. *Cf.* also *Appendix 1 — Various Signs in Music* for a detailed explantation.

dal segno (D.S.) This phrase (which means "to the sign" in Italian) is abbreviated *D.S.* It tells the player to jump forward or backward to a place in the music which is marked with the sign: 𝄋 . *Cf.* also *Appendix 1 — Various Signs in Music* for a detailed explantation.

dampen This means to stop a note from sustaining. *Cf.* also *sustain.*

D.C. *—cf. da capo*

decrescendo To decrescendo means to gradually play more and more softly. A decrescendo is often indicated by the composer but can be added by the player at his own discretion which helps create a more interesting and personalized interpretation. *Cf. Appendix 5 — Sample Staff Layout* for an example. *Cf.* also *crescendo.*

development This is a section of a piece where the composer begins to change the main theme (melody) to create more interest.

dexterity This means simply how nimbly the fingers are able to execute their work on an instrument.

diatonic Diatonic can be used as a noun defining a type of *scale (q.v.),* exercise, *etc.* It means that a musical element fits into a specific *key (q.v.).* *Cf.* also [2] *chromatic.*

diminished A note (usually in a chord) is said to be diminished when one of the notes is lowered one-half step further than is normal in a key. An *interval (q.v.)* may be diminished if it is lowered one-half step further than normal in a key. *Cf.* also *augmented.*

dissonant Two or more pitches (or even an entire piece) that sound unpleasant when played together are "dissonant." This is obviously a very subjective concept. It is the opposite of *consonant (q.v.).*

dominant —*cf. scale degrees*

dot A dot is placed next to a note to indicate that the note should sustain one-half of it's value longer than normal. *Cf. Appendix 5— Sample Staff Layout* for an example.

dotted This is a reference to a type of rhythm. If you are walking — right, left, right, left, *etc.*, this rhythm of your feet is "even." If you started to skip, this rhythm of your feet would sound uneven and is called "dotted."

1 **double bar** At the very end of a piece, rather than a single *bar line (q.v.)* there are *two* barlines (one thin and one heavy). This tells the player that the piece is finished. There can also be double bars written within a piece (both written with a *thin* line). This type of double bar divides one *section* from another. *Cf. Appendix 5 — Sample Staff Layout* for an example.

2 **double flat** A double flat is a *chromatic (q.v.)* sign that tells the player that the note immediately following the sign should be played, not only one half-step lower (*i.e.* "flatted"), but *two* half-steps lower. The sign for a double flat is ♭♭ .

3 **double sharp** A double sharp is a *chromatic (q.v.)* sign that tells the player that the note immediately following the sign should be played, not only one half-step higher (*i.e.* "sharped"), but *two* half-steps higher. The sign for a double sharp is 𝄪 .

4 **double stop** When a bowed string instrument plays two or more notes, this is referred to as a *double stop* (for two notes), a *triple stop* (for three notes) or a *quadruple stop* (for four notes).

1 **downbeat** This is the first beat of a composition, or a section of a composition. Normally you begin a piece (or a section) "on the downbeat" because it is a logical place to start, since it is the beginning of a musical idea — like starting to read a sentence at the beginning rather than in the middle.

2 **downbeat** A downbeat refers to the action given by a conductor to tell the players when a piece begins. It is different from a *cue (q.v.)* since a cue tells a player when he should make an *entrance (q.v.)* after the piece has already started.

down bow This is the term to indicate when the bow (of a violin, viola, cello or bass) is moving in the direction of the *frog (q.v.)* of the bow. It is indicated in the music by the sign: ⊓ . *Cf.* also *up bow.*

D.S. *cf. dal segno*

duo A *duo* is a musical piece to be performed by two people.

trio = for three people,
quartet = for four people,
quintet = for five people,
sextet = for six people,
septet = for seven people,
octet = for eight people,

...past that, a piece is usually referred to as a piece for "chamber music" *(q.v.)* or a piece "for ensemble."

duration The duration of a note is how long it is held or sustained before it is stopped from sounding. The duration of a rest is how long the silence should last before the next event in the music happens. *Cf.* also *sustain.*

dynamic(s) This is the relative loudness or softness (volume) of music. Dynamics are often indicated by the composer but can be added by the player at his own discretion, which helps create a more interesting and personalized interpretation. Dynamics are usually referred to in the plural form, since there is virtually always more than one dynamic in a composition. *Cf. Appendix 5 — Sample Staff Layout* for an example. *Cf.* also *Appendix 4 — Dynamics.*

— E —

ear training Ear training is a study that the teacher may include in lessons. It teaches the student to recognize different *intervals, chords (q.v.), etc.* when he hears them. In Europe (thus, for many teachers who have been trained there) a synonym for ear training is *solfège (q.v.).*

embellishment *—cf. ornament*

enharmonic Like a synonym in language, two notes that sound the same but are written differently are called enharmonic. For example C♯ and D♭ are actually the same pitch, but a composer will chose which way to *write* that pitch in the music depending on how he is developing a composition.

ending An ending in music refers to a specific series of signs (predominantly brackets and numbers) that tells the player how to proceed. Rather than create severe confusion, simply follow the numbers in the example below, and you'll easily understand the musical concept of endings. *Cf.* also *repeat sign.*

Fig. 9. Example of first and second endings.

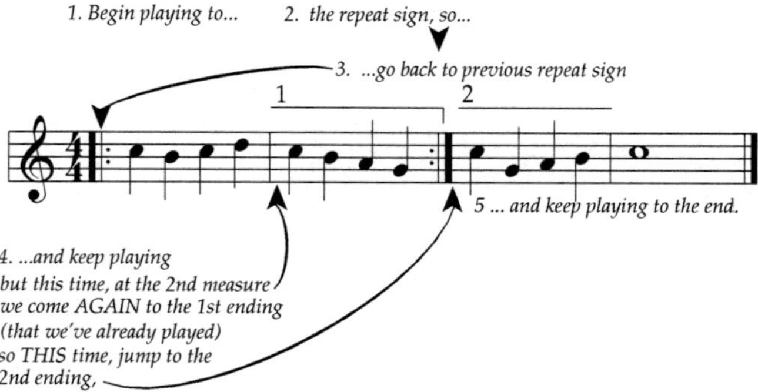

ensemble When musicians play together, they are playing in an ensemble. This is the opposite of *solo (q.v.)*. The word ensemble can also refer to a small group of musicians such as a string quartet, a quintet, *etc.* *Cf.* also *duo*

entrance An entrance is where and when a player begins playing. This is particularly important in *chamber music (q.v.)* because if an entrance is false (at the wrong time) it will not match with the other musicians. *Cf.* also *cue.*

ethnic music Virtually any music that has a strong nationalistic style or reflects a specific culture can be called ethnic music.

ethnomusicology This is a branch of *musicology (q.v.)* that studies the music of different cultures.

excerpt In orchestra music, obviously not everything each musician plays is the *solo (q.v.)* — sometimes it is simply *accompaniment (q.v.).* However when there is a solo it is usually a section that is more difficult and very important. Thus, many teachers will use excerpts (the more difficult, important sections of a large composition) — to teach orchestral instrumentalists. There are books of excerpts that give only these important solos from larger compositions.

expression marking This is the explantation at the very beginning of a piece that tells a player the relative *tempo (q.v.)* and mood of a composition. These are sometimes also given later in a piece if the mood changes. Expression markings are often in Italian, so you will need to have a large music dictionary to check the precise meaning. *Cf. Appendix 5 — Sample Staff Layout* for an example.

— F —

f-hole On the *table (q.v.)* (the top) of a violin, viola, cello or bass, there are two holes cut out in the form of a stylized letter "f." These are called the f-holes. They allow the air to move through the instrument so it can resonate more freely and amplify the sound. *Cf.* also *sound hole.*

facsimile A facsimile is a printed copy of a first or early edition of a composition. It can sometimes be an advantage for a student to study or play from a facsimile or *Urtext edition (q.v.)* rather than a modern edition of a piece, since some modern editors have changed (for the worse) parts of the original composition. *Cf.* also *manuscript.*

fair copy —*cf. manuscript*

felt The common material felt is used in a number of instruments. In the piano it is used on the *hammers (q.v.)* as well as on the *dampers (q.v.).* When buying a used piano, make sure to check the felt because if it is very old it may be hardened and/or moths may have eaten some of the felt and it will need to be replaced.

On many wind instruments (flute, clarinet, saxophone, *etc.*), felt is placed under the keys to make an air-tight seal between the key and the hole when the key is depressed. These need to be replaced periodically.

fermata This is a sign that tells the player to hold that note or chord longer than its written value. It is marked with the sign: 𝄐 . *Cf. Appendix 1 — Various Signs in Music* for a detailed explanation.

fine This Italian word means simply, "end." Pronounced "fē̄ē'-nā," it is written in music to tell a player where the final section (the "fine") is.

figure A figure is a small melody or rhythm that is very recognizable. Figures are important for the player to recognize in the music since they are often repeated throughout the piece. Obviously, if the player can comfortably play one figure, he can play it when it happens again, which saves time practicing.

figured bass Some teachers use figured bass to teach keyboard students. Normally all the notes are written out on the page, and you simply play what's written. However, figured bass (also called thorough bass) is "short hand" which gives an actual written bass line, but rather than all the other notes, there are a series of numbers written above or below the bass line that tell the player which chords should be played while he then *improvises (q.v.)* the other parts. This is a very old notational technique that can be a fascinating way for students to learn improvisation in a classical style of playing. *Cf.* below for an example of figured bass.

Fig. 10. Example of figured bass. [1]

fingerboard The left hand fingers are placed on a stringed instrument (to play different notes) on the fingerboard. This is different from the *keyboard (q.v.)* of a piano, organ, *etc.*

fingering The fingering is small numbers or letters (depending on the instrument) written near the notes to tell the player which fingers to use when playing specific notes. Teachers will usually be *very* strict that a student uses the correct fingering, since (especially in beginning studies) the correct fingering will help develop specific technical skills. *Cf. Appendix 5 — Sample Staff Layout* for an example.

first ending *—cf. ending*

flag A flag is the curved line drawn from the *stem (q.v.)* of a *note (q.v.)*. The number of flags tells the player the *duration (q.v.)* of a note. A flag may also be written as a *beam (q.v.)*. *Cf. Appendix 1 — Parts of a Written Note* for an example.

flat This sign looks like this ♭. It tells the player that the note with this sign should be played one half-step lower, *i.e.* the very next lowest note on the instrument. *Cf.* also *half step.*

---

1. Taken from Bach, C.P.E., *The True Art of Playing Keyboard Instruments (Versuch die wahre Art das Clavier zu Spielen,* Berlin, 1759), p. 282.

flutter tongue This is a special technique used on many wind instruments. Rather than playing a note (simply by blowing), the player plays the note normally, but rolls the tongue (as if he were saying a rolled "r" as in Spanish or French). This will be indicated in the music by the composer; *i.e.* it is never improvised.

footstool A footstool is used by classical and some jazz guitarists to raise the left leg higher than the right in order to make the playing position more comfortable. If the teacher suggests using a footstool, *make sure that the child practices at home using the footstool!!!*

form Every composition has a specific form. Musical form is similar to the different forms in poetry, such as a sonnet, a limerick, an ode, *etc.*

Recognizing the different musical forms makes the music easier to learn, because a student will understand where the sections begin or end as well as the style of the composition so he can work on one section after another and the practicing is more efficient.

The details of specific forms should be looked up in an expanded dictionary, but the more common forms include the following:

air (aire)
allemande
arabesque
aria
ballad
barcarole
bagatelle
bolero
bourée
branle
canary
canon
capriccio (caprice)
cavatina
chaconne (caconne)
choral
courante
cycle
dirge
double
elegy
étude (study)
fantasy (fantasie)
folia
fughetto
fugue
galliard
galop
gavotte
gigue (jig)
humoresque
hymn
impromptu
invention
lament
lied
march
mazurka
minuet
motet
nocturne
ode
partita
passacaglia
pavan
perigourdine
polka
polonaise
prelude
quadrille
ragtime
rapsody (rhapsody)
recitative
ricecar
ritornello
romance (romanza)
rondo
round dance (round)
rounded binary
sarabande
serenade
siciliana
sonata
sonata allegro
sonatina
suite
tango
tarantella
three-part song form (ternary)
toccata
tourdion
two-part song form (binary)
variations (theme and variations)
villanella
volta
waltz

frame A piano has a metal frame which helps support the construction of the instrument. The frame design will greatly affect the sound of the instrument. Be sure and ask the teacher or music store salesperson to explain the construction of the frame of any piano you are considering buying.

fret A fret is the little metal band that extends across the *fingerboard (q.v.)* of a guitar, banjo, *etc.* Be sure to check *every* note on *every* fret on *every* string when buying an instrument, since frets that are too low or high will make the notes either rattle or not sound.

frog This is the rectangle-shaped piece of wood (sometimes of ivory) at the end of a bow (for violin, *etc.*) where you hold the bow with the right hand. The opposite end of the bow is called the *point (q.v.).*

fugue This is a musical *form (q.v.)* using the compositional technique of *counterpoint (q.v.).* It is essentially the same as the round, *Row, Row, Row Your Boat,* but instead of playing two lines at the same time, there can be *many* more lines played at the same time, often turned upside-down, backwards, *etc.* Fugues are popular in teaching because the player learns many specific techniques.

— G —

grace note A grace note (more properly called an *appoggiatura*) is the most common type of *ornament (q.v.)*. How it is played depends on the historical period, but the teacher will explain how a grace note should be performed on the specific instrument. A grace note may be either ascending or descending. In general, grace notes are written as shown below.

Fig. 11. Examples of written grace notes (the smaller notes).

(Ascending grace note)

(Descending grace note)

gauge The gauge of a string means how dense it is. For example, a heavier gauge will usually produce a louder sound, but the tension of the string will also be tighter which can make it more difficult to play. The teacher will suggest a specific gauge of strings for a specific instrument and the strength of a specific student's hands. *Always buy the gauge and brand of the string recommended by the teacher!*

grain The grain of the wood of any wooden instrument will greatly affect the sound. Be sure to ask the teacher or music store salesperson to explain the different woods and different grains of the wood when buying an instrument.

— H —

hammer In a piano, the hammer is a felt-covered piece of wood that strikes the strings when a key on the keyboard is depressed. When buying a used piano, be sure to check the condition of hammers, since if they are very old, they may be too hard which can give the piano a harsh and brittle sound. *Cf.* also *felt.*

half step Imagine one note, then imagine the very next lowest or highest note possible. The distance between these two is a half step. *Cf.* also *whole step.*

harmony The harmony of a piece is essentially the musical background for the melody. The study of harmony, is one aspect of *music theory (q.v.)* and can be very complicated. Don't feel as though you should understand it all, but the teacher will probably teach some basic aspects of music theory (including the study of harmony) to your child.

[1] **head** The head of a stringed instrument is that part furthest from the body of the instrument where the strings are tuned. *N.B.* the very end of the head of a violin, viola, *etc.*, is called the *scroll (q.v.)* while the actual area that holds the pegs is called the *peg box. (q.v.).*

[2] **head joint** When you disassemble a flute, the section where you blow is the head joint.

— I —

iconography This is a field of study in *musicology (q.v.)*. It is the study of music through historical pictures, paintings and sculpture. In studying artworks from a historical period, we can learn a great deal about how people played music, the types of instruments they used, *etc.* There are many beautifully published books that can be fascinating for students to look through, which can help develop their interest in music history and different instruments.

imitation This is a compositional technique used in *counterpoint, fugues (q.v.),* and many other styles of composition. In imitation, a melody, rhythm, or some other recognizable part of the music is repeated (*i.e.* "imitated").

improvise Usually music is written specifically as to which notes, rhythms, *etc.* should be played. Some musicians (in rock, jazz, *etc.*) will improvise, *i.e.* they will make up their own melodies or harmonies to fit with a piece.

inlay The inlay on an instrument is the fancy material (usually wood, ivory, mother of pearl, *etc.*) around the edge or other parts of an instrument. Inlay is purely cosmetic and does absolutely nothing to improve the sound of an instrument, but often more expensive instruments will have more inlay. *Cf.* also *purfling.*

interpretation This is the individual way that a performer performs a work. It is a result of combining the *articulation, timbre, dynamics* and *phrasing (q.v.)* into the performance of a piece.

interval The distance between two notes (played separately or together) is an interval. There are many different types of intervals (because of the many possible distances between two notes). The study of intervals, is one aspect of *music theory (q.v.)* and can be very complicated. Don't feel as though you should understand it all, but the teacher will probably teach some basic aspects of music theory (including the study of intervals) to your child.

intonation If a player or an instrument produces a very exact pitch the intonation is "correct." If not, the intonation is incorrect or "false." Obviously for some instruments (piano, *etc.*) the player can do nothing to change the intonation, while on other instruments (flute, violin, *etc.*) the intonation is a very important part of learning the instrument. Be sure to have the teacher or an instrument repairman check the intonation of an instrument that you are considering buying.

—J—

jam Musicians who *improvise (q.v.)* often meet to play together in order to "jam," implying improvising together. Jam may be used as both a noun ("to have a jam" or a "jam session") or it can be used as a verb ("...we're going to jam"). The word is traditionally used in jazz music.

jazz Jazz is a specific style of music. In it's most basic form, a "head" (the main melody) is played by one or more musicians, then each one begins to *improvise (q.v.)* different melodies and/or rhythms while the other players continue playing the main melody or harmony. There are many forms of jazz (such as Dixieland Jazz, Free-form Jazz, *etc.*), each with fairly specific rules as to how one improvises.

— K —

[1] **key** A composition is written in a specific key. This basically means that it begins and ends on the same chord and some chords in that key will be more important than others. Different keys have a different numbers of *sharps* or *flats (q.v.)* so that the piece sounds correct.

[2] **key change** If the composer decides that he wants to change the mood of a piece, he can compose a new section so that different chords become more important. This makes the composition more interesting.

[3] **key signature** This is the collection of *sharps* or *flats (q.v.)* (or lack thereof) at the beginning of each *staff (q.v.)* in the music. It tells the musician which notes to raise (if a sharp) or which to lower (if a flat) so the piece sounds correct. *Cf. Appendix 5 — Sample Staff Layout* for an example.

keyboard The part of a piano, organ, *etc.* on which the fingers are placed to play different notes is called the keyboard. This is different from the *fingerboard (q.v.)* of a stringed instrument. The term *keyboard instrument* is also used as a general term meaning any instrument with a keyboard, such as piano, organ, harpsichord, clavichord, *etc.*

— L —

laminate As in furniture building, lamination means gluing two pieces of wood flat together for strength. Often the sides and back of a stringed instrument are laminated (which doesn't greatly affect the sound), however the *soundboard (q.v.)* should usually not be laminated since a solid (non-laminated) soundboard usually produces the best sound. Inexpensive instruments usually have laminated soundboards. Be sure and discuss this with the teacher or music store salesperson when buying an instrument.

leading tone *—cf. scale degrees*

ledger line The 5 *lines* and 4 *spaces (q.v.)* make up a *staff (q.v.)*, but if a note needs to be written higher or lower than these, additional small lines can be added above or below the staff for each individual note. These are called ledger lines. *Cf. Appendix 5 — Sample Staff Layout* for an example.

legato This word may be used both as an adverb and noun. As an adverb, to "play legato" means to play smoothly, *i.e.* one plays from note-to-note with no noticeable break between the notes. This is as if you took one breath and sang several notes without taking another breath; the notes run together. *Cf.* also *staccato,* which is the opposite of legato.

As a noun, the term legato is used in 19th century music to imply a *slur (q,v,).* In 19th century classical guitar music, it is also used to mean bringing the fingers of the left hand down on the fingerboard very quickly (without using the right hand to pluck the string) to produce the note. This is different from a *slur (q.v.),* when the right hand plucks a string and the left hand changes fingers to get two different notes. With a 19th century guitar legato, *only* the left hand is used.

In both cases, when written, a legato is usually indicated by a broad phrase marking (the arch) as shown below.

Fig. 12. Example of legato marking.

line A staff has 5 *lines* and 4 *spaces (q.v.)*. Each indicates to the musician a different note to play.

luthier A luthier is a person who makes small instruments (violin, guitar, *etc.*). A *builder (q.v.)* builds larger instruments. *Cf.* also *builder*.

— M —

main theme Every piece has a melody presented at the very beginning that is the most important of the composition. This is the main theme. In some compositional styles, this may also be called the *subject (q.v.).* Some pieces also have another, slightly less-important theme called a sub-theme, or secondary theme.

major The composer will decide which *key (q.v.)* a piece should be written in. This is indicated by the *key signature (q.v.).* In addition, he will decide if that key should be major (happy sounding) or minor (sad sounding). *Cf.* also *minor.*

manual A manual on an organ or harpsichord means simply a *keyboard (q.v.).* If you notice on the organ at church, there are usually at least two different identical keyboards. Some organs have as many as five manuals and each one can be preset to play a different set of pipes or effects which makes it easier for the organist to change quickly from one sound to another.

manuscript Just like in writing a book, a musical manuscript is the handwritten version the composer sets down on paper as he composes. It can be interesting for intermediate and advanced students to study manuscripts because they can see how a composer develops his ideas, which gives some insight as to how he thinks. *Facsimile (q.v.)* copies of manuscripts by many famous composers are available for sale and can also look beautiful as framed art.

There are several types of manuscripts:

autograph manuscript: a hand written copy made by someone other than the composer, but signed ("autographed") by the composer to verify that it is a correct version of the finished composition.

fair copy: a finished version of a composition written in the composer's own hand.

working manuscript (also called a sketch): the basic (often unfinished) manuscript written by the composer in his own handwriting. These often contain different musical ideas scribbled as he developed the work. Working manuscripts can be the most fun to study (or hang on your wall!) because they often include coffee stains, shopping lists scribbled on the margins or (in the case of my own compositional manuscripts) telephone numbers of people I was supposed to call, but forgot the all-important names of the people...

measure This is the section in the music between the *bar lines (q.v.). Cf. Appendix 5— Sample Staff Layout* for an example.

measure line *—cf. bar line*

mediant *—cf. scale degrees*

metronome A metronome is a mechanical device invented by Dietrich Nikolaus Winkel in Amsterdam around 1812, but the idea was taken and further developed by Johann Maelzel shortly thereafter. It is a pendulum device that gives a clicking sound and may be adjusted to sound a specific number of beats per minute. Beethoven was the first composer to use a metronome to indicate the exact *tempo (q.v.)* of his pieces.

Teachers often insist that students practice warm-ups or exercises with a metronome to make sure the playing is steady and even. While you can still buy a wind-up metronome, the modern battery-operated are usually more practical and just as inexpensive.

The marking "M.M." at the beginning of a piece originally meant "Maelzel Metronome," but has erroneously come to mean "metronome marking." *Cf. Appendix 5 — Sample Staff Layout* for an example.

metronome marking (abbreviated M.M.) This is a misnomer for "Maelzel Metronome." *Cf. metronome.* This often appears at the beginning of a piece. It indicates the exact *tempo (q.v.)* (speed) of the composition. *Cf. Appendix 5 — Sample Staff Layout* for an example.

minor The composer will decide which *key (q.v.)* a piece should be written in. This is indicated by the *key signature (q.v.).* In addition, he will decide if that key should be major (happy sounding) or minor (sad sounding). *Cf.* also *major.*

mode Today, we normally use two types of *keys (q.v.): major* and *minor (q.v.).* In some music, especially from the Middle Ages and some *ethnic music (q.v.),* there are many other different types of keys, called modes. If you listen to a Gregorian Chant, you will notice that it sounds very different from our modern type of music. Much of this is because these medieval chants use different modes that are rarely heard today.

modulation A modulation occurs in the music when the composer decides he wants to write part of the piece in a different *key (q.v.); i.e.* he modulates to another key. He does this by changing some of the *notes* and *harmony (q.v.)* so that the piece (usually in a few measures) is in the new key. It's not much different from singing *Mary Had a Little Lamb* starting on one note, then singing the second verse starting on a different note, except a composer usually tries to do this so the modulation to the new key is very smooth and unnoticeable.

monophonic Monophonic music is music (usually from an older historical period such as the Middle Ages) that has a predominant single melody (with no other accompaniment or other melodies). In general, this style developed into *polyphonic music (q.v.).*

motive A motive is a small melody or a small part of a melody. Composers will use a motive over and over in a composition because it is small and easily recognized by the listener, thus more interesting.

mouthpiece A mouthpiece is the very end of wind instruments where you blow.

[1] **music dictation** This is exactly like a secretary taking dictation, but in this case the teacher will sing or play a melody or rhythm and the student will write it on *staff paper (q.v.).* This is an important aspect of *ear training (q.v.).* It teaches the student to recognize different *rhythms, intervals, chords, (q.v.), etc.* when he hears them.

[2] **music history** Exactly as the name implies, this is the study of the history of music. It is usually in reference to the history of western music, although it can include *ethnomusicology (q.v.),* the history of musical style (the ways different composers wrote music), *etc.* The study of music history, even at an elementary level, is a critical part of musical studies.

[3] **music theory** This is the study of how music works. It can be *incredibly* involved. It is possible to earn a Ph.D. in music theory, so don't feel as though you should understand it all, but the teacher will probably teach some basic aspects of music theory to your child.

[4] **music therapy** This is a fascinating study and application of music whereby playing or singing is used as a tool to relax, help develop certain motor or cognitive skills, *etc.* Many hospitals and even large corporations have a music therapist to work with their patients, employees or staff.

musicology This, in the broadest sense of the term, is the study of *everything* historical about music. It includes *music history (q.v.), music theory (q.v.), ethnomusicology (q.v.), music pedagogy* and *performance practice (q.v.).*

mute A mute is a device that fits somewhere on an instrument to alter the sound. There are different types of mutes for various instruments. For example, instruments such as a trumpet have a whisper mute (that fits into the *bell (q.v.)* to make it sound very quiet and metallic; a cardboard mute to make the sound very quiet and less harsh.

Instruments such as the violin have a mute (usually of wood) that is placed on the *bridge (q.v.)* to give it a quiet and slightly "nasal" sound; a practice mute (often of metal) makes the instrument very quiet.

There are also "special effects" which qualify as mutes. Some contemporary compositions (even for beginners) require the player to construct his own mute. For example on the classical guitar, foam rubber can be placed under the strings next to the bridge for a dramatic effect; a soft rag may be placed in the end of a flute, *etc.*

Little-by-little, you may find yourself buying mutes at the suggestion of the teacher. They are usually inexpensive and last for years.

Note that the term mute can be used both as a noun (as above) or as a verb: "to mute" means to either use a mute or to *dampen (q.v.)* the strings; *i.e.* to stop them from ringing.

— N —

natural This sign looks like this ♮. It tells the player that the note with this sign should be returned to its original pitch, usually after the same note which had been altered by a *sharp* or *flat (q.v.).*

neck Like the part of your body, the neck of a stringed instrument is the long part between the *body* and the *head (q.v.).* In buying an instrument it is critical that the neck is very straight (not warped or twisted) and that it is a comfortable length and width for the student's hands.

[1] **note** A note conveys two pieces of information to the musician:

1) *how* it is written — the shape of the *note head (q.v.)* and if there are any *flags (q.v.)* or *beams (q.v.)* — will indicate how long the note should sustain;

2) *where* it is written on the *staff (q.v.)* will indicate which note should be played.

Cf. Appendix 1 — Parts of a Note for an example.

N.B. The term note indicates a specific *written* sound while a *pitch (q.v.)* indicates a specific *aural* sound.

[2] **note head** A note head is the round part of a note (either solid or hollow). The shape of the note head tells the player the *duration (q.v.)* of a note (how long it should sustain). *Cf. Appendix 1 — Parts of a Note* for an example.

nut The strings pass over the nut at the *head (q.v.)* of a stringed instrument. *Cf.* also *bridge.*

— O —

oblique (motion) —*cf. contrary motion*

octave If you look at *Appendix 3—Notes on the Staff,* you will notice that the notes go from C (followed by D, E, F, G, A, B) and then begin again at C. Any note that has the same name, but is written higher or lower on the *staff (q.v.)* may be one octave, two octaves, three octaves, *etc.* from the original.

octet —*cf. duo*

off-beat Usually the beats of a rhythm are even, as if you were walking, left, right, *etc.* If the beats fall between this normal pattern, they are called off-beat.

opus This Italian word simply means "a work." You find it a lot in the titles of classical music because some older composers (instead of giving a piece a name, such as "The Moonlight Sonata," or "The Brandenburg Concerto") would simply list their compositions as *Opus Number 1, Opus Number 2, etc.* This tells you at least the order in which the pieces were composed, but (I agree) it makes for some pretty boring titles!

Note that some composers (particularly very old composers) will have different numbering systems, usually named for a musicologist who has done a lot of research on their music.

For example, Wolfgang Amadeus Mozart's works are listed as K. 100, K. 200 (spoken as "Köchel Number One hundred," *etc.)* named after Köchel, one of Mozart's biographers. Johann Sebastian Bach's works are listed as B.W.V., meaning *Bach-Werke Verzeichnis* (in English, "Bach's Catalog of Works").

By the late 19th century, most composers began giving their pieces names as well as using opus numbers. This makes it possible to know in which order they were written, as well as being a lot more interesting.

orchestration In essence, this is an *arrangement (q.v.)* of a piece for orchestra, which was written either by the composer himself or by someone else. It also refers to a composer's tendency to write so that one instrument sounds more important than another which will give a specific "style" to a composer's works.

This is much of what differentiates the sound of one composer's music from that of another. *Cf.* also *arrangement, transcription.*

ordinario —*cf. timbre*

ornament An ornament (also called an embellishment) is one or more notes added by the player at specific points in the music to make it more interesting. Ornaments are either indicated by the composer or they can be improvised by the performer. There are many rules for the use of ornaments, depending on the historical period, style, composition, *etc. Cf. Appendix 1 — Various Signs in Music* for an example.

ostinato An ostinato is a rhythmic pattern that recurs over and over in a piece.

overtone When you hear one note, called the fundamental, you are also hearing many other, almost inaudible notes, at the same time above that single note. These other notes occur in a specific order and are called overtones.

Different instruments have some overtones that are louder than others, which is one of the main reasons that instruments sound different from one another.

Overtones have very little to do with playing an instrument, but this overtone series is one of the main reasons that one instrument will sound brighter while another will sound darker.

— P —

pad A pad is the soft material, usually made of a type of *felt (q.v.)* underneath the keys of many wind instruments to help make an air-tight closure when the key is depressed. It is important that the pads are not too worn, otherwise air will leak and the note will not be clear. Be sure and check the pads when buying a wind instrument. You will need to have new pads put on an instrument by a woodwind repairman every year or so.

parallel (motion) *—cf. contrary motion*

part A composition that is for two or more people normally has the music printed and bound separately for each person. This separate booklet of music is called a part. *Cf.* also *score,* in which all the parts are printed together on one page.

passage This is a small section from a piece. Students will usually practice an entire passage in practicing, since it has a specific beginning and ending, thus, it sounds logical when played in it's entirety.

pedagogy This simply means the study of how to teach.

[1] **pedal** Many instruments have pedals. They refer specifically to the part of an instrument where you use your feet, such as the pedals on a piano, harp, organ, *etc.*

On the piano there are three main pedals:

1) damper pedal (also called the *sustaining pedal):* (to the far right): This allows the pianist to play a note, depress the pedal, and release the note (which would normally cut the sound), but because the sustaining pedal is depressed, all the notes continue sustaining.

2) una corda pedal (also called the *soft pedal):* (to the far left) This pedal shifts the *hammers (q.v.)* slightly to one side so that not all of the strings are hit by the hammer, thus the sound is softer.

3) sostenuto pedal: (in the middle) *N.B.* This pedal does not exist on all pianos. It allows the player to sustain only those notes whose dampers have already been raised: *i.e.* the player can sustain single notes while the hands play other (non-sustaining) sections.

On an organ, the foot pedals play actual pitches while on a harp the pedals stretch or release tension on specific strings so that they play different notes that wouldn't otherwise be available.

[2] **pedal point** This term comes from organ playing where sometimes a very low note (played with the foot pedals) is held for a long time while the rest of the music continues over the top. In composition (as shown below) a pedal point is a note that is held over an extended period while other activity continues in the upper parts. A pedal point is similar to a pedal tone, but a *pedal point* is usually in reference to one instrument, while a *pedal tone* is in reference to several instruments (the lowest one of which is playing the pedal point).

Fig. 13. Example of a pedal point. [2]

pedaling This noun refers to the indications in the music that tell a pianist when to depress and release a specific pedal. The most common pedaling signs are given below. *Cf.* also *Appendix 1—Parts of a Note and Various Signs in Music.*

Ped. = depress pedal
❋ = release pedal

peg box This is the part of a violin, viola, *etc.*, where the pegs (which are used to tune the instrument) are located. It is similar to the *head (q.v.)* of a guitar, lute, *etc.*

perfect pitch A person has perfect pitch if he can hear specific pitches, movements in a melody and harmony and know *exactly* what pitches are involved. Some people seem to be born with perfect pitch, though it can be learned. It is similar to *relative pitch (q.v.).*

---

2. From: Bach, Johann Sebastian, *Two-Part Invention, No. 7,* measures 15-17.

performance practice Each historical period has different rules for how music should be played. The performance practice of a historical period is the process of applying those rules when playing so the music sounds as it was originally intended by the composer.

phrase If a *beat (q.v.)* can be equated to a letter, and a *measure (q.v.)* to a word, then a phrase is like a sentence. It is one, complete musical idea.

phrasing This is a critical aspect of interpretation. It is the general way a player shapes a musical line as he plays. It is similar to the way we enunciate words as we speak a sentence. Phrasing is often indicated by the composer but can be added by the player at his own discretion, thus helping to create a more interesting and personalized interpretation.

piano reduction If a large composition (such as for orchestra) is rewritten so it can be played on the piano, that printed music is called a piano reduction.

pick-up —*cf. anacrusis*

piston This is the part inside a trumpet, and other brass instruments, that goes up and down when you press a key. In buying an instrument (especially if it is used), it is critical to make sure the pistons are clean. To check the pistons, you unscrew the joint directly under the key.

Some older instruments are corroded so you can't unscrew this joint to get the piston out. Do *not* buy such an instrument! French horns have a different type of piston called a *rotary valve (q.v.)*.

[1] **pitch** This is the highness or lowness of a note. *N.B.* The term pitch indicates a specific *aural* sound while a *note (q.v.)* indicates a specific *written* sound.

[2] **pitch pipe** This is a little contraption that you blow into (sort of like a harmonica) which produces specific pitches. It can be used to find the correct pitch when singing, or to tune an instrument, though most teachers prefer that a student learns to tune with a *tuning fork (q.v.)*, since it is more accurate.

point This is the pointed end of a bow (for violin, *etc.*). The opposite end of the bow is called the *frog (q.v.)*.

ponticello —*cf. timbre*

polyphonic Polyphonic music is music (usually from an older historical period such as the late Middle Ages or Renaissance) that has more than one melody. In general, this style developed from *monophonic music (q.v.)*.

prepared In contemporary music, this is a compositional style which requires that the instrument be "prepared." You may hear the phrase prepared piano, prepared guitar, *etc.* In this style, different objects are attached to the instrument or strings (such as fishing lead, clamps, pieces of paper, *etc.*). These objects drastically change the sound and make for a variety of special effects.

purfling The purfling is the *inlay (q.v.)* (usually wood, mother of pearl, *etc.*) that is glued around the outer edge of an instrument (*i.e.* guitar, violin, *etc.*). Purfling is purely cosmetic and does absolutely nothing to improve the sound of an instrument, but often expensive instruments will have more detailed purfling. *Cf.* also *inlay*.

— Q —

quadruple stop —*cf. double stop*

quartet —*cf. duo*

question —*cf. consequent*

quill A quill is the part of a harpsichord that plucks the string when a key is depressed. It is similar to a *hammer (q.v.)* on a modern piano (since it sounds the string) but a hammer *hits* the string, while a quill *plucks* the string.

quintet —*cf. duo*

— R —

range This is how high and how low notes can be sung or played on an instrument. This total range is usually divided up into specific sections or "registers." *Cf.* also *register.*

realization Sometimes a piece is written in *figured bass (q.v.),* or only sketched by a composer or editor, and the player must figure out what he wants to specifically play. The player's version of that piece would be his realization. This differs from a *transcription (q.v.),* which is a piece that has been rewritten for another instrument.

recital A recital is a concert, but for only one or two musicians.

reed A reed is usually made of *cane (q.v.)* and is the part of many wind instruments (clarinet, oboe, *etc.*) that vibrates to produce the pitch when you blow in the *mouthpiece (q.v.).*

register Each instrument or voice has a *range (q.v.)* which is the total of the notes (low to high) that can be played or sung. However, this total range (depending on the instrument) is often divided up into sections, since specific sections of the overall range have different characteristics. Often, the lower register has a darker *timbre (q.v.)* while the middle register has a more neutral timbre, and the upper register may have a pinched or nasal timbre.

For example, all the notes that a singer can physically sing would be the range, but each voice has generally three different registers: head (the higher notes), throat (the middle notes) and chest (the lower notes).

Instruments also have specific registers and each produces a specific type of sound.

relative pitch A person has relative pitch if he can hear specific movements in a melody or harmony and knows what the movements are, but he can't tell you specifically which *pitch* it is. Some people seem to be born with relative pitch, though it can be learned. It is similar to *perfect pitch (q.v.).*

repeat sign A repeat sign (as shown below) tells the player to go back to the previous repeat sign one time, then continue further. *Cf.* also *Appendix 1— Various Signs in Music.*

Fig. 14. Example of a repeat sign.

repertoire A musicians repertoire means simply the pieces that he plays and/or has the ability to play on short notice. It is important that a student maintain a repertoire of pieces (preferably from memory) so that he can perform when the opportunity arrises.

resolution When a melody or harmony comes to an end, it is at a resolution. A resolution occurs at a *cadence (q.v.)* but can also be written anywhere into a composition to give a momentary sense of relaxation.

rest A rest is a sign written in the music to indicate when nothing should be played; *i.e.* it indicates a specific *duration (q.v.)* of silence. Unlike a note, a rest conveys only *one* piece of information to the musician: *how* it is written (the shape, *etc.*) will indicate how long the silence should last. *Cf. Appendix 2 — Rhythms* for examples.

rhythm The rhythm is the different combinations of beats between two or more notes.

rib Commonly called a brace, a rib is a piece of wood inside a wooden instrument (violin, guitar, *etc.*) that runs around the body of the instrument securing the back and the sides, and between the *table (q.v.)* and the sides.

A rib does two things:

1) it helps support the construction of the instrument, *and*

2) it helps transfer the vibration of the sound through the wood so the instrument sounds louder.

In buying any wooden instrument (especially if it is used) it is important to check that the ribs are not loose, since that will cause the instrument to rattle and/or it will have an inferior sound. If the ribs are loose, they can usually be glued by a repairman. *Cf.* also *brace.*

ritard (abbreviated: *rit.*—pronounced *ri-tard'* [*N.B.* accent is on second syllable]) A ritard is when the player gradually plays more and more slowly. It can occur at the end of a *phrase (q.v.)* and often at the end of an entire composition before the final *cadence (q.v.)*.

Ritards are an element of *interpretation (q.v.)* and may be written into the music by the composer or added by the player at his own discretion, which helps create a more interesting and personalized interpretation.

rotary valve This is the part inside a French horn that moves when you press a key. In buying an instrument (especially if it is used), it is critical to make sure the valves are clean. To check the pistons, you unscrew the joint directly under the key. Some older instruments are corroded so you can't unscrew this joint to get to the valves. Do *not* buy such an instrument! The same rule applies for buying any brass instrument. Trumpets, *etc.* have a different type of valve called a *piston (q.v.)*.

run This is a popular word for a fast scale or melody. Students will often practice runs over and over because they are usually more difficult and faster than the surrounding sections.

— S —

sacred music This is music that was written specifically for use in the church. *Cf.* also *secular music.*

[1] **scale** A scale is simply a series of notes in a specific order, with a specific distance between each note. *Scales* and *arpeggios (q.v.)* are often used as *warm-ups (q.v.).*

[2] **scale degrees** This refers to specific names that are sometimes used to indicate notes in a scale. The advantage of using these names is that they refer to relative position in a *key (q.v.)* rather than to a specific note.

For example in the key of C, the note C = the first tone, the note D = the second tone, *etc.* However in the key of D, the note D = the first tone, the note E = the second tone, *etc.* They are obviously all different.

However, by using the names of scale degrees instead of the names of specific notes, you can name any position of a note (regardless of the key), and not need to refer to a specific note.

In order, the scale degrees are:

1st scale degree	=	tonic
2nd scale degree	=	supertonic
3rd scale degree	=	mediant
4th scale degree	=	subdominant
5th scale degree	=	dominant
6th scale degree	=	submediant
7th scale degree	=	leading tone (*or* subtonic)

[3] **scale length** The scale length is simply how long the neck is on an instrument with a *neck (q.v.)* (guitar, violin, *etc.*). In buying an instrument, it is critical that the scale length be neither too short (which causes the student to cramp the hands), nor too long (which causes the student to have to reach too far for certain movements).

score Music that is for two or more musicians has the *parts (q.v.)* printed and bound separately. On the other hand, a score is the printed music that has *all* the different parts printed together. This is what a conductor looks at when conducting an orchestra, *etc.*

An example of one page of an orchestral score is given below.

Fig. 15. Example of a score for orchestra. [3]

3. From: Glise Anthony, *"The Globe Rooms," Concerto No. 1 for Guitar and Orchestra, Op, 11* (St. Joseph/Vienna: Ævia Publications, 1989). Performance Rights: BMI. Used by Permission.

scroll The scroll of a bowed stringed instrument (violin, viola, 'cello, and bass) is at the very tip of the *head (q.v.)*. It is the carving that looks a bit like a snail. The area directly next to the scroll which holds the pegs is called the *peg box (q.v.)*.

second ending *—cf. ending*

secondary theme *—cf. sub theme*

secular music This is music that was written specifically for use outside of the church. *Cf.* also *sacred music.*

septet *—cf. duo*

serial music Also called twelve-tone music, this is a contemporary style of composition using a series of notes (thus the word "serial") in a very strict manner.

sextet *—cf. duo*

sharp This sign looks like this ♯. It tells the player that the note with this sign should be played one half-step higher, *i.e.* the very next highest note on the instrument. *Cf.* also *half step.*

sketch *—cf. manuscript*

slide This is the part of a trombone that moves back and forth to play different notes. It is critical that this moves freely.

slur Normally, notes are played somewhat separately the same way we speak and make a slight distinction between each word. When there is a slur between two or more notes, it indicates that those notes should be played or sung without separately sounding each of the notes.

This is similar to a liaison between two words of speech; you hear the distinct pitches, but they are run together with no noticeable break.

The sign for a slur is an arc which looks identical to the sign for a *tie (q.v.)*, but a slur is between *different* notes while a tie is between *identical* notes. *Cf. Appendix 5 — Sample Staff Layout* for an example.

solfege This word comes from French (solfège) and implies the learning of pitch names, rhythms and basic elements of *music theory* *(q.v.). Cf.* also *ear training,* which is virtually the only aspect of traditional French solfège that is taught in the U.S.

solo When one musician plays by himself or has the most important part in *chamber music (q.v.),* he is the soloist, playing a solo. This is the opposite of *ensemble (q.v.)* playing.

soprano *—cf. voice*

soundboard Also called the "table," this is the top part of the *body (q.v.)* of a stringed instrument (guitar, violin, piano, *etc.*) over which the strings are stretched. With most instruments, the wood used on the sides and back are not too important, however the soundboard is critical, since this is the part of the instrument that vibrates the most. In buying an instrument, be sure and have the teacher or music store salesperson explain the construction of the soundboard on the specific instrument you are considering buying.

Each type of wood used for a soundboard will have different characteristics that will radically effect the sound. In general, the soundboard should be solid — *i.e.* not *laminated (q.v.),* and the *grain (q.v.)* should be straight and fairly close together.

soundbox The hollow part inside the body of an instrument (guitar, violin, *etc.*) is called the soundbox. The shape of this resonating space will affect the sound, as will the *braces (q.v.)* in the soundbox. Be sure and have the teacher or music store salesperson explain the construction of the soundbox and the bracing system.

[1] **sound hole** A sound hole is the open (usually round) hole on the front *[table (q.v.)]* of a guitar. It's function is the same as the *f-holes (q.v.)* on a violin, in that it allows the air to move more freely through the *soundbox (q.v.),* thus making the instrument vibrate more freely and amplify the sound.

[2] **sound post** A sound post is a small, round-shaped piece of wood inside a violin, viola, cello or bass. It extends from the *soundboard (q.v.)* to the back. This is one of the most important parts inside these instruments. In French a sound post is called the "âme" or "soul" — which indicates it's importance. It is *never* glued into place, but wedged tightly between the soundboard and the back inside the instrument. Where the sound post is placed is a virtual science and will drastically alter the sound of an instrument. In buying an instrument, always have

the teacher or a repairman check the sound post and *bass bar (q.v.)* since a loose soundpost or bass bar can make even a fantastic instrument sound terrible.

space A staff has 5 *lines* and 4 *spaces (q.v.).* Each indicates to the musician a different note to play.

staccato This word may be used both as a verb and noun. As a verb, to "play staccato" means to play with a distinct separation between each note, *i.e.* one plays from note-to-note with a noticeable break between the notes. This is as if you took one breath and sang one note then quickly took another breath for the next, another for the next, *etc.;* the notes would sound very separate.

A staccato (or staccato marking) as a noun is a small dot placed above or below the note head which indicates that the note should be played separated from the surrounding notes. *Cf.* also *legato,* which is the opposite of staccato.

Fig. 16. Example of written staccatos.

1 **staff** This is the diagram of 5 *lines* and 4 *spaces (q.v.)* where the notes are written.

2 **staff paper** Your child will use staff paper frequently in lessons. It is printed with the *staff (q.v.)* blank so the teacher can write in additional music (often exercises), or the student will use this paper for *music dictation (q.v.), etc.* It is usually a good idea to buy a booklet of staff paper which is bound so the sheets will stay in a specific order.

stem A stem is the straight line drawn up or down from the *notehead* of a *note (q.v.). Cf. Appendix 1 — Parts of a Written Note* for an example.

stop A stop on an organ is above the *keyboard (q.v.)* and is either pulled or is a switch that you press to activate different pipes or effects on the instrument. There can be dozens of stops on an organ.

straight Two or more notes, when played at the same time, are played straight — *i.e.* they are not played *broken* or *arpeggiated (q.v.)*.

subdominant —*cf. scale degrees*

submediant —*cf. scale degrees*

sub theme Every piece has a melody, presented at the very beginning, which is the most important part of the composition. This is the main theme. However, some pieces also have another, slightly less-important theme called a sub-theme, or secondary theme. *Cf.* also *main theme.*

subtonic —*cf. scale degrees*

subject This is the main melody of a composition.

[1] **sul ponticello** —*cf. timbre*

[2] **sul tasto** —*cf. timbre*

supertonic —*cf. scale degrees*

sustain When one or more notes continue sounding, they are sustained. This is the opposite of *dampened (q.v.)*.

syncopation A rhythm is syncopated when it does not fall evenly in the normal rhythmic pattern of a piece. For example, the rhythmic structure of much ragtime music is syncopated.

system In a *score (q.v.),* one entire section printed across the page is referred to as a system.

— T —

tablature In the Middle Ages, through the Renaissance, some music (specifically for organ, lute, guitar and a few other instruments) was written in tablature. This is a system where different letters or numbers tell the player where to put the fingers for specific notes. For example, Renaissance English lute tablature had 6 lines (used to represent the six strings), and each *fret (q.v.)* (where you placed the left hand fingers) was indicated by a letter — a, meant the string was played open, b, was for the first fret, c, for the second fret, *etc.*

Tablature has again become popular in folk and rock music, since it provides guitarists who can't read music an opportunity to learn pieces that have very specific notes. 0 = an open string; 1 = the first fret; 2 = the second fret, *etc.*

Most serious teachers *strongly* disapprove of using tablature, since it takes nearly as long to learn tablature as it does to learn traditional note reading and the student is severely limited, since he can *only* play music that is written in tablature. Tablature also has severe limitations, since it is impossible to notate how long notes should *sustain (q.v.)*, and specific fingerings (that are critical in more advanced music) are difficult to notate. All these problems are the reasons that tablature was abandoned over 500 years ago for our modern notation.

Fig. 17. Example of modern guitar notation (above) with corresponding guitar tablature (below). [4]

IV Nova

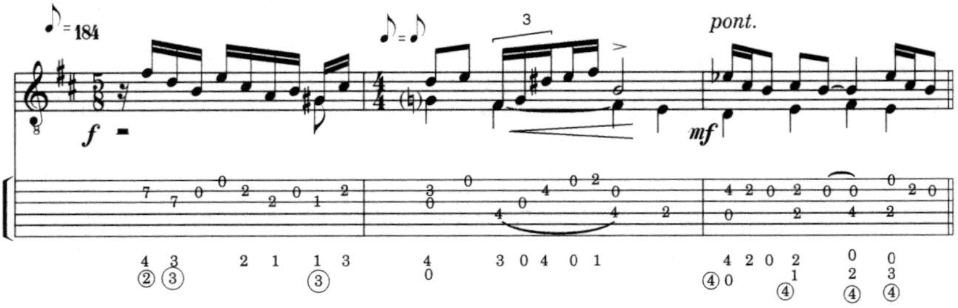

4. From: Glise, Anthony, "Nova" from *The Canonization, Sonata No. 2 for Solo Guitar, Op. 7, measures 1-3.* (St. Joseph/Vienna: Ævia Publication, Ltd.) 1994. © 1994 by A. Glise. All Rights Reserved. International Copyright Secured. Performance Rights: BMI. Used by Permission.

table —*cf. soundboard*

tasto —*cf. timbre*

technique Technique refers to how well a musician can execute the music on his instrument. *Scales* and *arpeggios (q.v.)* are technical studies which are almost always a part of the daily *warm-ups (q.v.),* since they prepare the fingers to play pieces and help develop specific technical abilities.

tempo This is the speed at which a piece is played.

texture The texture of a composition refers to how "heavy" or "light" it sounds. This is obviously a very subjective asthetic judgement, but it is strongly influenced by the *voicing (q.v.)* of a composition.

theory —*cf. music theory*

thorough bass —*cf. figured bass*

tie A tie is written between two (or more) identical notes. It indicates that the second note should not be re-played, rather, it is *sustained (q.v.).* The two notes are played as if they were written simply as one note.

The sign for a tie is an arc which looks identical to the sign for a *slur (q.v.),* but a tie is between two identical notes while a slur is between different notes. *Cf. Appendix 5 — Sample Staff Layout* for an example.

timbre (pronounced to rhyme with the word *amber*) On some instruments, the same note can be made to change the timber (sometimes also called the "tone color"). The note is the same, but it sounds brighter or darker. For example, sing the letter *e* with your mouth wide open as if you were smiling. Then keep singing the same note while you gradually shape your mouth to form a small circle. The different relative sound between the two is the timbre. Timbre is often indicated by the composer but can be added by the player at his own discretion which helps create a more interesting and personalized interpretation.

The more common names used for timbre variants are given below:

ordinario (abv. *ord*)	=	play normally (where the right hand or bow would normally play)

sul tasto	=	with a darker timbre (play with the right hand or bow nearer to the fingerboard)
sul ponticello	=	with a brighter timbre (play with the right hand or bow nearer to the bridge)

[1] **time change** Normally a composition begins with a specific *time signature (q.v.)* and this doesn't change. However, many contemporary and *ethnic (q.v.)* styles of music will change the time signature throughout the piece to create a special rhythmic effect. When this happens it is called a time change.

[2] **time signature** These are the "fractions" written at the very beginning of a piece. A time signature is spoken simply as two numbers (starting with the top number) *i.e.* a time signature of 3/4 would be spoken as "three-four," *not* "three-fourths."

The top number tells the musician how many beats there are in each measure. For example, if the top number is 3, you would evenly count, "one, two, three." Then you would be at the end of the measure and you would continue counting over again as you go to the next measure. Note that the counting always remains steady and even; you don't slow down or stop between measures. It's a bit like skiing (particularly if you ski as poorly as I do) — once you start moving, there's no stopping until you get to the end!

The bottom number of the time signature tells the musician which note to count as one entire beat. If it were a 4, that would mean you count a quarter note as one beat. If it were an 8, it means you count an eighth note as one beat, *etc. Cf. Appendix 5 — Sample Staff Layout* for an example.

tonality The tonality of a piece means simply what *key (q.v.)* it is written in.

tone color This is the same as *timbre (q.v.)*, but most professional musicians will use the word timbre as opposed to tone color.

tonic —*cf. scale degrees*

tonguing Most wind instruments produce *very* different sounds if the player uses or shapes his tongue in different ways as he plays a note. For example, if a flutist makes the sound "paah," as he plays, he produces a very different sound than when he makes the sound "tee." These various articulations on wind instruments are referred to as tonguing.

transcription If a piece is written for one instrument, but someone rewrites it for another instrument, that piece is referred to as a transcription.

transposition A transposition is a composition that was originally in one key and rewritten to another key. It's much the same thing as making a translation of a story from one language to another; the meaning and ideas are the same, but the sound is different. *Cf.* also *arrangement; orchestration.*

trio *—cf. duo*

triple stop *—cf. double stop*

tuning fork This is a two-pronged piece of metal that gives one specific pitch when you strike it. It is used to find a pitch when singing or to tune an instrument. Because it is very accurate, most teachers prefer that a student learn to tune using a tuning fork, rather than a *pitch pipe (q.v.)*. However, a tuning fork is more difficult to learn to use because it gives only one pitch.

twelve tone music *—cf. serial music*

— U —

up bow This is the term used to indicate when the bow of a violin, viola, cello or bass is moving in the direction of the *point (q.v.)* of the bow. It is indicated in the music by the sign: V . *Cf.* also *down bow.*

upbeat —*cf. anacrusis*

Urtext (edition) This word comes from German, thus, since it is a noun, it is always capitalized. It translates *Ur* (original) *text* (copy or text). An Urtext edition of music is one that has been copied directly from the original, but typeset again — not printed directly from the original itself as a *facsimile (q.v.).*

It can sometimes be an advantage for a student to study or play from an Urtext or facsimile edition rather than a modern edition of a piece, since some modern editors have changed (for the worse) parts of the original composition.

— V —

value The value of a note is simply it's duration; how long it sustains.

valve —*cf. piston; rotary valve*

vibrato A vibrato is a slight "tremble" in a pitch that is (in modern times) added by a player at his own discretion. For example, on the violin, it is done by very slightly rocking the playing finger back and forth.

vocal attacks In singing, there are *many* different ways to articulate a note. For example, singing a note with more force in the throat, with more emphasis from the nasal area, *etc.* These various types of *articulations* and *timbres (q.v.)* in singing are referred to as vocal attacks.

voices Just as each person has different physical characteristics, each singer has a different type of voice. These types are usually defined by their *range (q.v.)*, meaning how high or low they can sing. The basic voice types are listed below from high to low.

soprano (women)
alto (women)
tenor (men)
baritone (men)
bass (men)

voicing The voicing of a composition means how the notes (which are played at the same time) are spaced: "closed," which means closely together, or "open," which means further apart. The voicing will drastically effect the sound of a composition. More closed voicing can sound "heavy," while more open voicing can sound "lighter."

— W —

warm up Used as a noun, this is a study or piece used to loosen the fingers so the player is more prepared to play. As a verb, a player "warms up" when he is playing through a study to prepare to play.

whole step Imagine a note, then imagine the very next highest, then the very next highest above that one. The distance between the first and last note is a whole step.

working manuscript *—cf. manuscript*

wound string For many stringed instruments, the lower sounding strings (called the bass strings) are often wound, meaning that, rather than being a solid piece of material, they have an inner core which is wound (usually with metal) to create an even thicker string. The materials and type of wound string will usually be recommended by the teacher to suit the instrument and the level of the student's expertise.

No critical entries

youth orchestra A youth orchestra is traditionally a local orchestra (often organized through a college or conservatory) which meets once a week to learn *repertoire (q.v.)* and give the players performing experience. If the teacher suggests that your child play in a youth orchestra, *do it!* This can be a tremendous learning experience and the interaction with other young musicians can be a very positive inspiration.

No critical entries

Appendices

- Appendix 1 — *Parts of a Note and Various Signs in Music*
- Appendix 2 — *Rhythms*
- Appendix 3 — *Notes on the Staff*
- Appendix 4 — *Dynamics*
- Appendix 5 — *Sample Staff Layout*

Appendix 1 — Parts of a Note and Various Signs in Music

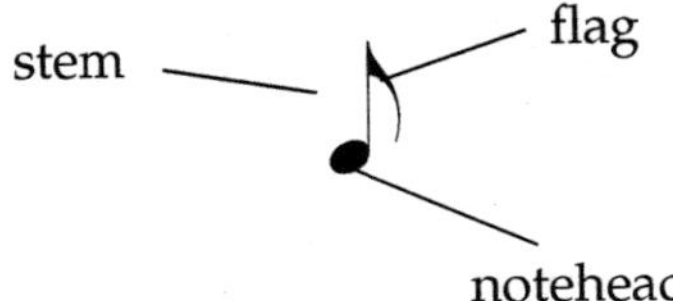

N.B. Notes may be written with the stem either up or down. Sometimes notes are written with the flags together as a beam. The concept is however still the same as if they were written with the flags drawn separately; *i.e.* one flag or beam is an eighth note, two flags or beams is a sixteenth note, *etc.* *Cf. Appendix 2* for a detailed explanation.

Various Signs in Music

This is a *roll* sign. Used for guitar, piano, harp and any instrument that can play more than one note at once. It indicates that two or more notes which are written together (*i.e.* on top of each other), should be played with a slight separation, usually from the lowest note to the highest.

A *fermata* ("pause" in Italian) may be written either up or down (as shown) and is placed over or under a note to indicate that you should hold the note longer than the written value.

Up-bow and *down-bow* signs tell a violinist and other bowed instrumentalists which direction the bow should be moving.

8va 8vb

An octave sign tells the player that he should play the same notes as written, but either an octave higher or an octave lower than written.

A *comma* indicates when to take a breath.

Repeat signs indicate a section to play again.

A *segno* sign ("sign" in Italian) tells the player that he should play to the measure where *"del segno"* is written, then to jump forward or backward in the piece to this sign and continue playing from that point.

A *coda* sign ("tail" in Italian) indicates the final section of a piece. Since you often jump forward to this section from somewhere else, it is marked with this sign to help the player find it easily on the page.

A *pedal* sign tells a pianist when to depress a pedal.

This sign has no particular name, but is used to tell a pianist when to release a pedal.

This sign is placed in the middle of a measure that doesn't have any notes and tells the musician to play exactly the same thing as he did in the previous measure.

The following signs are for different ornaments. Defining the execution of ornaments is *far* beyond the scope of this book, but I have listed them by name so if the student forgets what the teacher told him to do, you can look these up in a music dictionary.

 grace note

 turn

 mordent

 half trill

tr. trill

Appendix 2— Rhythms

Notes	*Corresponding Rests*
= whole note. This should sustain for four counts.	whole rest
= half note. This should sustain for two counts.	half rest
= quarter note. This should sustain for one count.	quarter rest
= eighth note. This should sustain for 1/2 count. (two or more may be written with beams rather than with flags:)	eighth rest
= sixteenth note. This should sustain for 1/4 count. (two or more may be written with beams rather than with flags:)	sixteenth rest

N.B. It is possible to place a dot after any note/rest (*ex.* .). This increases the value (duration) of that note/rest by one-half the value of the original. It is then referred to as a "dotted half-note," "dotted quarter note," *etc*. Thus a half note (which usually receives 2 counts), with a dot (as shown above) would receive one-half of the original value *in addition to the original two counts;* thus it sustains for *three* counts.

Note also that, in theory, the notes continue *ad infinatum*. The next subdivision would be a 32nd- note, then 64th-note, then 128th-note, *etc*. For beginners, the rhythms probably won't go beyond 16th-notes, though in practice (especially in slow 18th century pieces) 128th-notes do sometimes appear.

Appendix 3 — Notes on the Staff

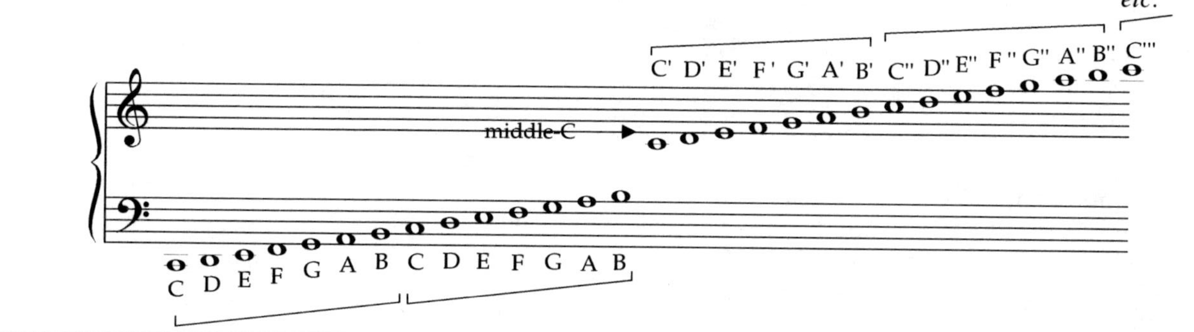

N.B. It is possible to have a flat sign or a sharp sign before any of the notes above. This would raise or lower that note by one-half step. One would simply say "C-sharp," "B-flat," *etc.* for the altered note. Double sharps and flats are also possible. These raise or lower the note by 2 half steps. Examples are shown below.

The musical scale goes from A to G, and then begins again with A. In practice, we say the name of the note and do not distinguish *which* we mean. In theory, the notes extend down to the point that they simply become a grumble, or so high that only dolphins could hear the pitch. The range given here is the most commonly used.

Example notations of:

Appendix 4—Dynamics

Dynamics (*i.e.* the general volume at which music is played) logically range from very quiet to very loud. Unfortunately, most dynamics are written in abbreviations that are from Italian, so unless you speak Italian, this "logical" system may not do you much good and you'll simply have to memorize the list below:

musical sign		the term in Italian		the meaning in English
pp	=	*pianissimo*	=	very quiet [1]
p	=	*piano*	=	quiet
mp	=	*mezzo piano*	=	moderately quiet
mf	=	*mezzo forte*	=	moderately loud
f	=	*forte*	=	loud
ff	=	*fortissimo*	=	very loud

Additional dynamic signs in music

sub.p	=	*subito piano*	=	suddenly quiet
sf or ***sfz***	=	*sforzando*	=	suddenly loud with a strong attack
fp	=	*forte-piano*	=	suddenly loud, then immediately suddenly quiet
sfp	=	*sforzando-piano*	=	suddenly loud with an attack, then immediately suddenly quiet

1. *N.B.* There also exists ***ppp*** (very, very quiet) and ***fff*** (very very loud). In fact, you can go, in theory, as far as ***pppp*** (very, very, very quiet) and ***ffff*** (very, very, very loud), but these are *extremely* rare in student literature and most composers consider these dynamic markings to simply be an over-done version of dynamics.

Appendix 5—Sample Staff Layout

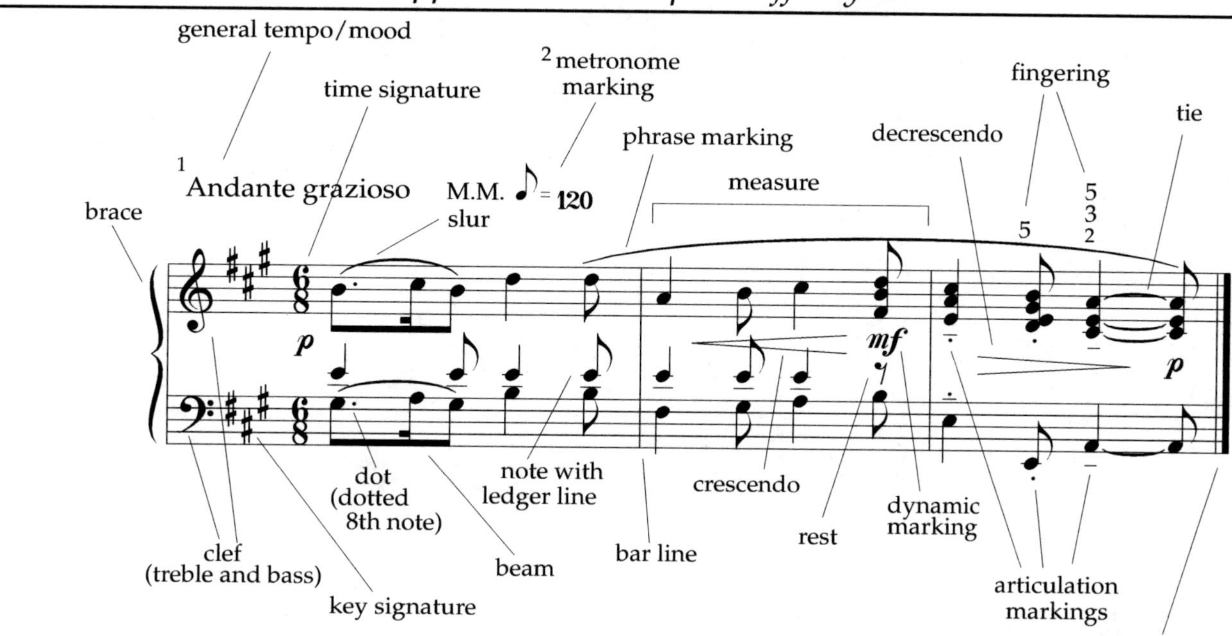

1. This example is adapted from the "Theme" from *Sonata No. 9 in A Major*, measures 6-8, by W. A. Mozart.
2. M.M. stands for "Maelzel's Metronome" (named for Johannes Maelzel who developed the contraption). A metronome makes a clicking sound at a specific speed, measured by the number of clicks per minute. In this case, the ♪ = 120 means there should be 120 eighth notes per minute. *Cf. metronome* in the glossary.

Author's Biography

The only American-born guitarist to win First Prize at the *International Toscanini Competition* (Italy), Anthony Glise is a product of the *Konservatorium der Stadt* (Vienna) and *New England Conservatory* (Boston) with additional study at the *Université Catholique de Lille* (France), *Harvard University* and *Accademia degli Studi "L'Ottocento"* (Italy).

Anthony gives periodic seminars on early music education for parents and children in the U.S., Germany, Italy, Austria and France. In addition to his concert work and university teaching, he still maintains a highly-select studio of particularly talented young classical guitarists, many of whom began their studies with him from the age of 5.

A *Pulitzer Prize Nominee* for composition, Anthony has performed and been awarded diplomas at such festivals as *Ville Sable* (France), the *ARCUM Festival* (Rome), *Festival Hautecombe* (France) and the *Nemzetközi Gitárfesztivál* (Hungary). In addition to traditional classical repertoire, his concerts often include 19th century works performed on a priceless 1828 Staufer Viennese guitar.

Anthony's commitment to the art has led to many diversified activities. His writings have been published extensively in *The Soundboard* (U.S.), *Guitar International* (England) and *Gitarre und Laute* (Germany). He has acted as an *Artist-in-Residence* and *Touring Artist* for a number of U.S. state arts councils and similar European programs. He is also the editor of the internationally-acclaimed series of guitar music, *"The Anthony Glise Editions,"* published by Willis Music Company and *"The Anthony Glise Urtext Editions"* by Mel Bay Publications, Inc.

An active composer, Anthony's original compositions have been premiered in such cities as New York, Chicago, Rome, Vienna, Lille (France) and Esztergom (Hungary).

His recordings include traditional works (solo, chamber, orchestral and ballet) as well as original compositions for such labels as Éclipse (France), Young Recording Artists (USA) and Dorian Recordings (USA). His first recording, *Overview,* was chosen as one of the year's "Top-5 Classical Releases" by *Vienna Life Magazine* in Austria.

Anthony lectures at the *Academy for the Study of 19th-Century Music* (Italy). When not on tour, he lives and teaches part-time in the Flanders region of Northern France and part-time in the US.

for more information, see: www.AnthonyGlise.com

Selected critiques...

"Anthony Glise offers us a totally different 'rhétorique' than we normally hear; his is a language of delicate effects, pure sensitivity, and contemplative emotions."

"The playing and sonority of Glise is not only clear and varied: it's a highly individual and spirited voyage."

"His style is not only that of power and decisive virtuosity: Glise seduces us by the grace and emotional intelligence of the phrase."

Le Diapason
(Paris, France)

"......so rich,
so profound,
so sensual,
that every note
tells a story."

Luister
(Amsterdam, Holland)

"...pure musical genius."

Classica
(Rome, Italy)

"Glise's playing is strikingly individual and blends an unbelievable dynamic range and ravishing tonal colors."

"Seldom have I been so impressed."

Vienna Life Magazine
(Vienna, Austria)

"...Glise has produced (rediscovered?) a radically different way of playing the guitar. His constantly evolving articulation makes every phrase a revelation. His fastidious attention to phrasing creates a *chiaroscuro* effect that I have only heard from the very best pianists or lute players."

"...a revelation, and should be heard by any guitarist who wishes to play 'expressively'."

The Soundboard
(Guitar Foundation of America)

Artist's Biography

Lucinda Weaver's artwork has been exhibited and published world-wide. Her custom art business, *"Quail Hollow Artworks,"* ® was founded in 1969 and has been the catalyst for producing over 800 original works. Many of these have been published as framed art, limited editions and notecards. Her fascination with American history has resulted in a lifelong commitment to local, Northern-Missouri themes, which are frequently exhibited and sold at festivals and galleries.

Just as the musician uses notes, Ms. Weaver considers a single line capable of conveying a message, while the quality and arrangement of a collection of lines can tell a story.

A specialist in pen and ink, her repertoire includes fine art drawings and calligraphy, as well as technical anatomical drawings, which appeared in Mr. Glise's university textbook, *Classical Guitar Pedagogy* (Mel Bay Publications, 1997).

Ms. Weaver's university training initially led to teaching art in high school, where she was affectionately dubbed "Weave" by her students (one of whom was Mr. Glise). Her longstanding commitment to developing friendship through art has produced an enormous network of friends and colleagues—many of whom have achieved highly active careers in the arts thanks to her influence.

Upon leaving the teaching force, she accepted her current position with the *St. Joseph Parks, Recreation and Civic Facilities Department* in St. Joseph, Missouri, where she is responsible for artistic design and layout of their various events and activities.

She is also a founding member of the *Sacred Hills Encampment,* a weekend living-history festival celebrating the rich heritage of Northwest Missouri.

A dynamic private art teacher, Ms. Weaver lives on a farm named *Whistle Creek* near St. Joseph, which was homesteaded by her family in the 1800's. When not busy with art students, fine arts projects, farming, and dairy cows, she and her husband and their three miniature schnauzers relax in the Rocky Mountains of Northern Colorado.